CASANOVA

erotica

SONIA HENSLER

Mastodon Publishing
Thoughts Made Real

ISBN 978-1-7320091-8-9 Printed in the United States

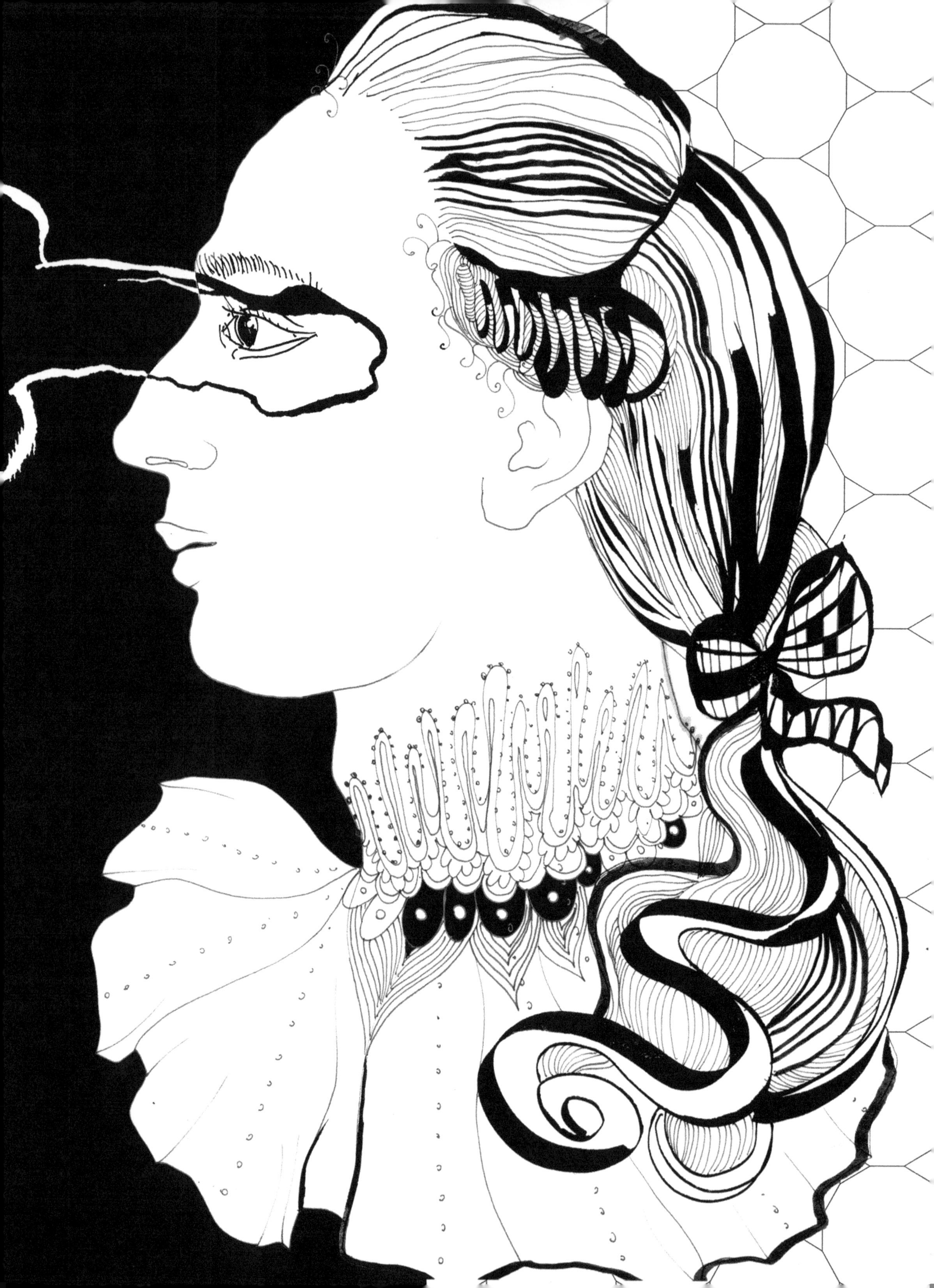

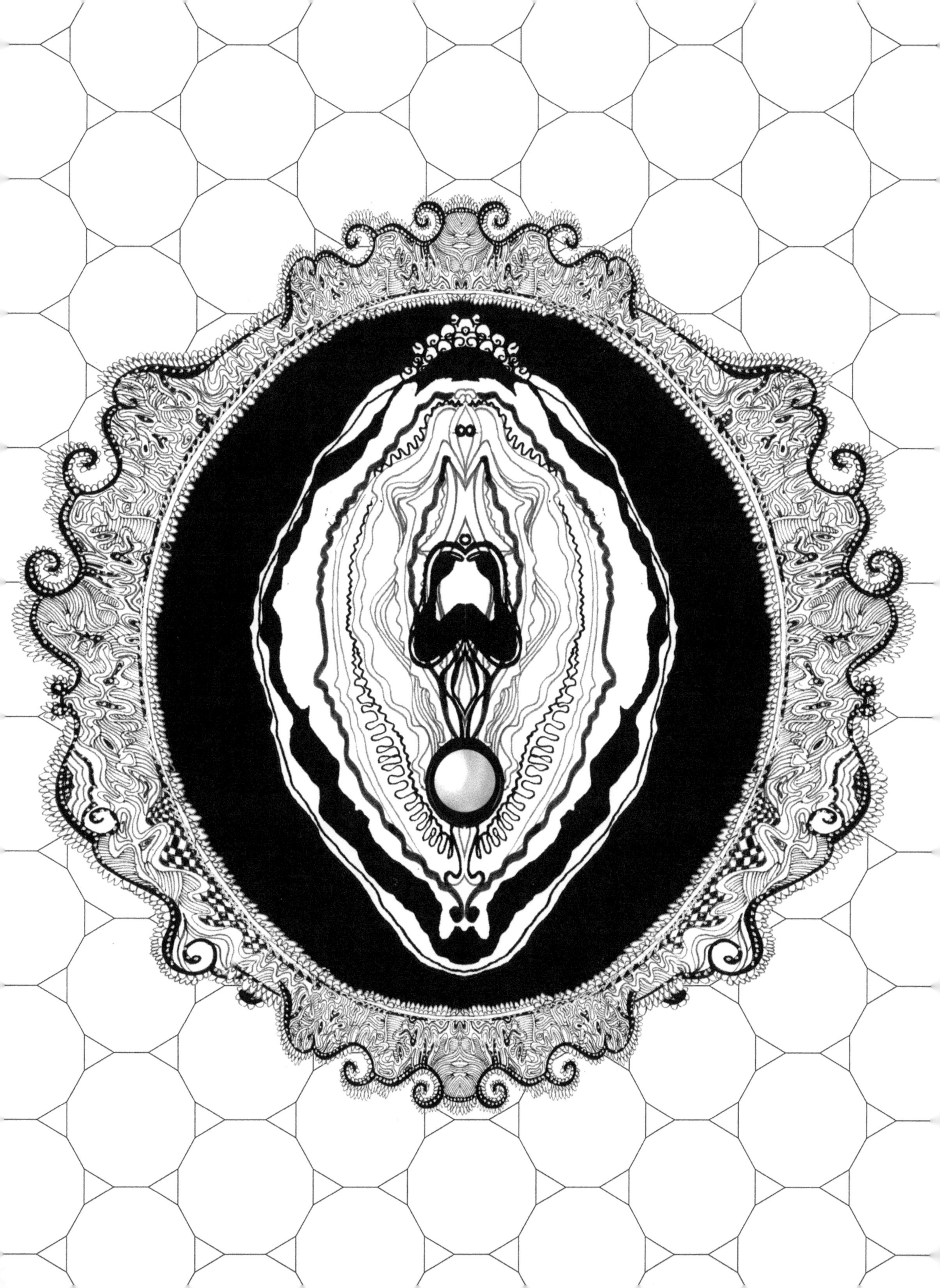

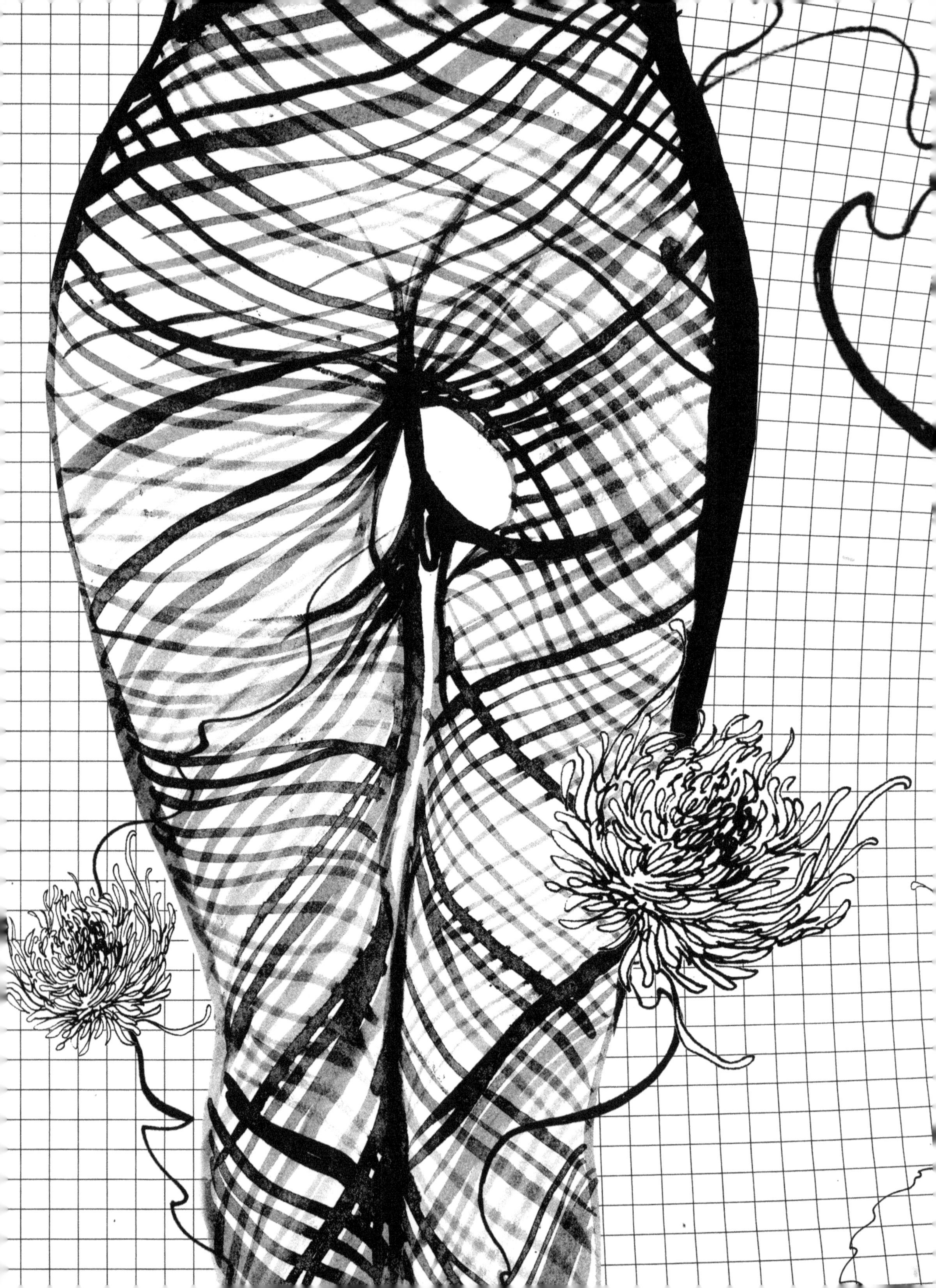

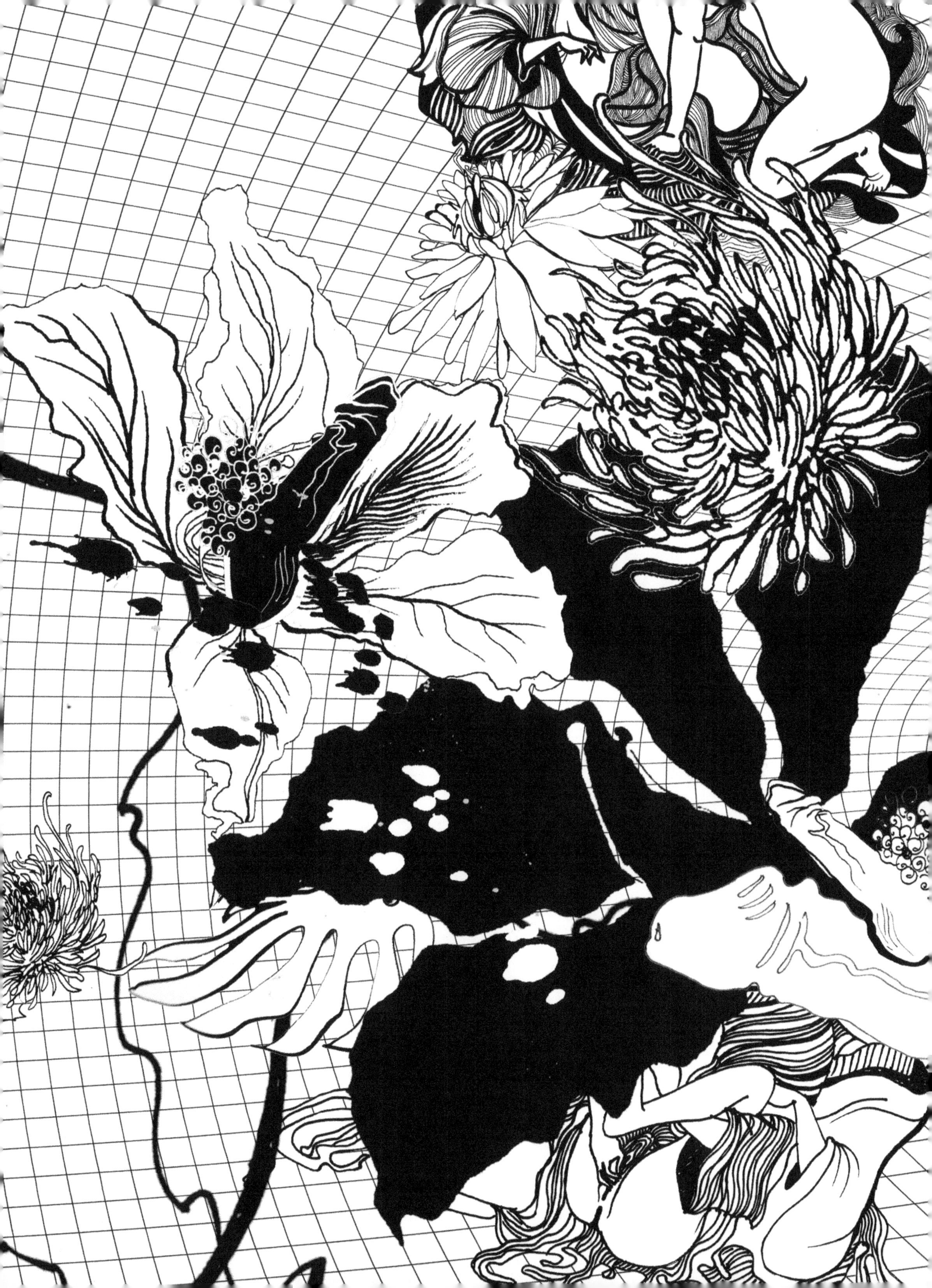

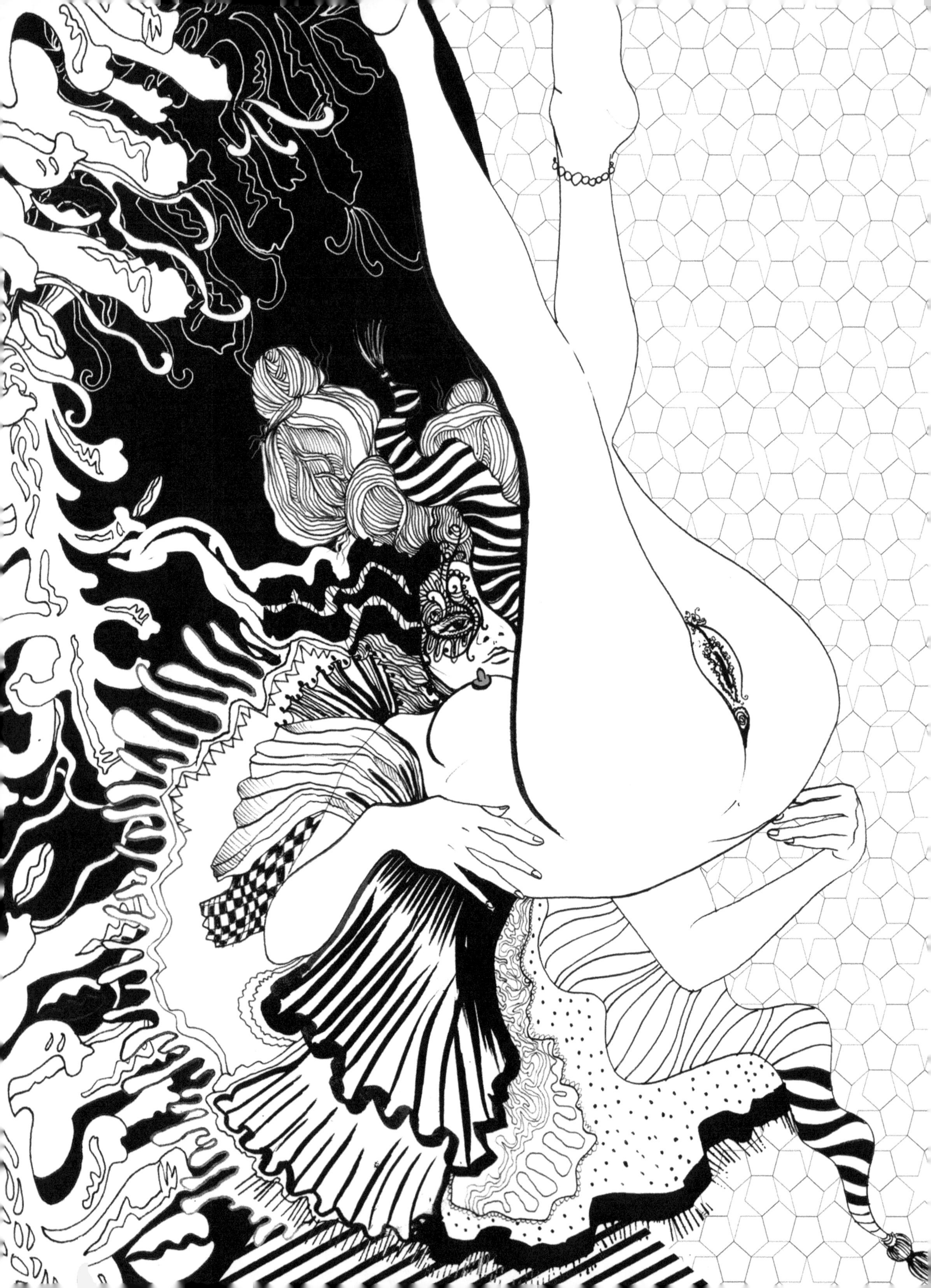

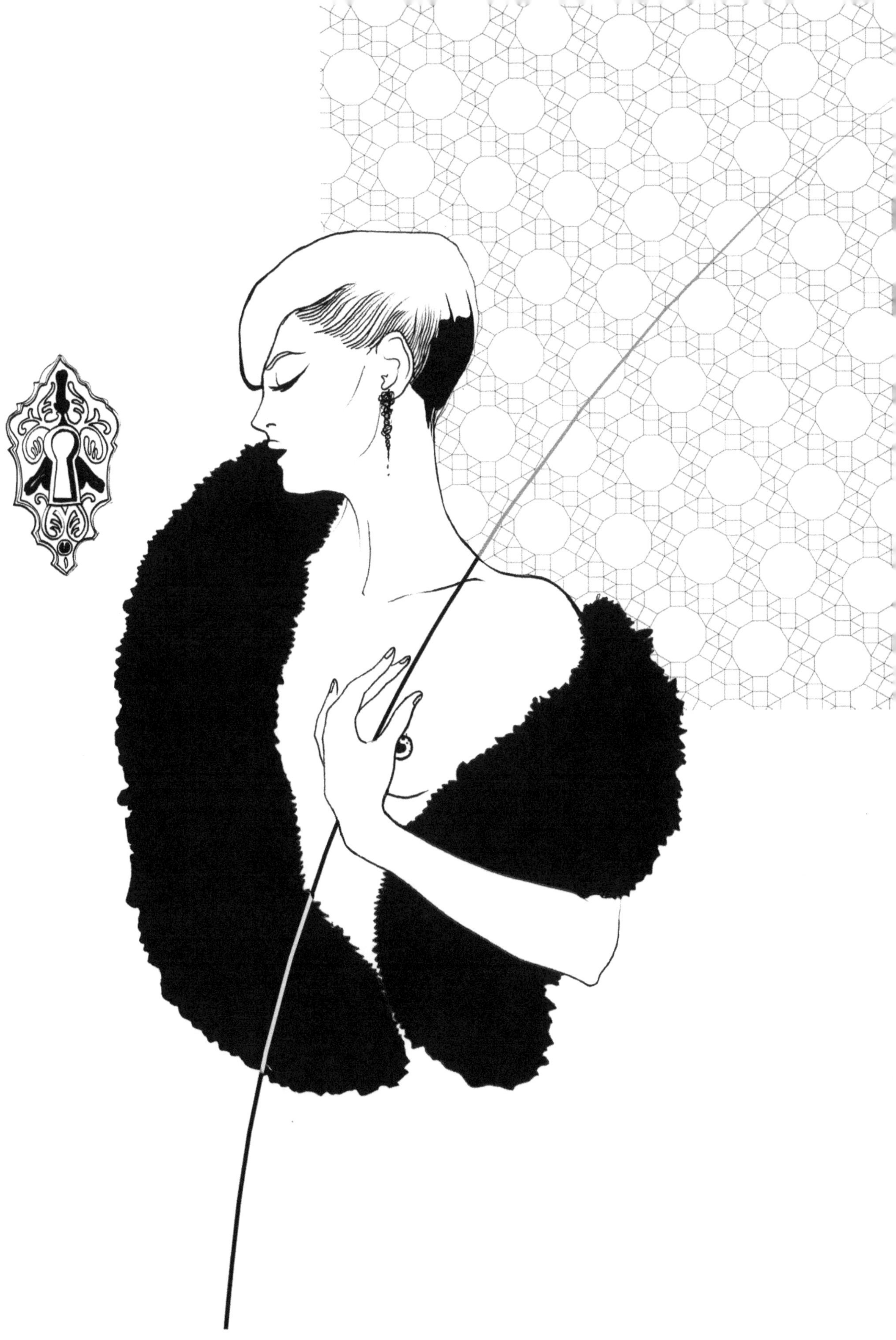

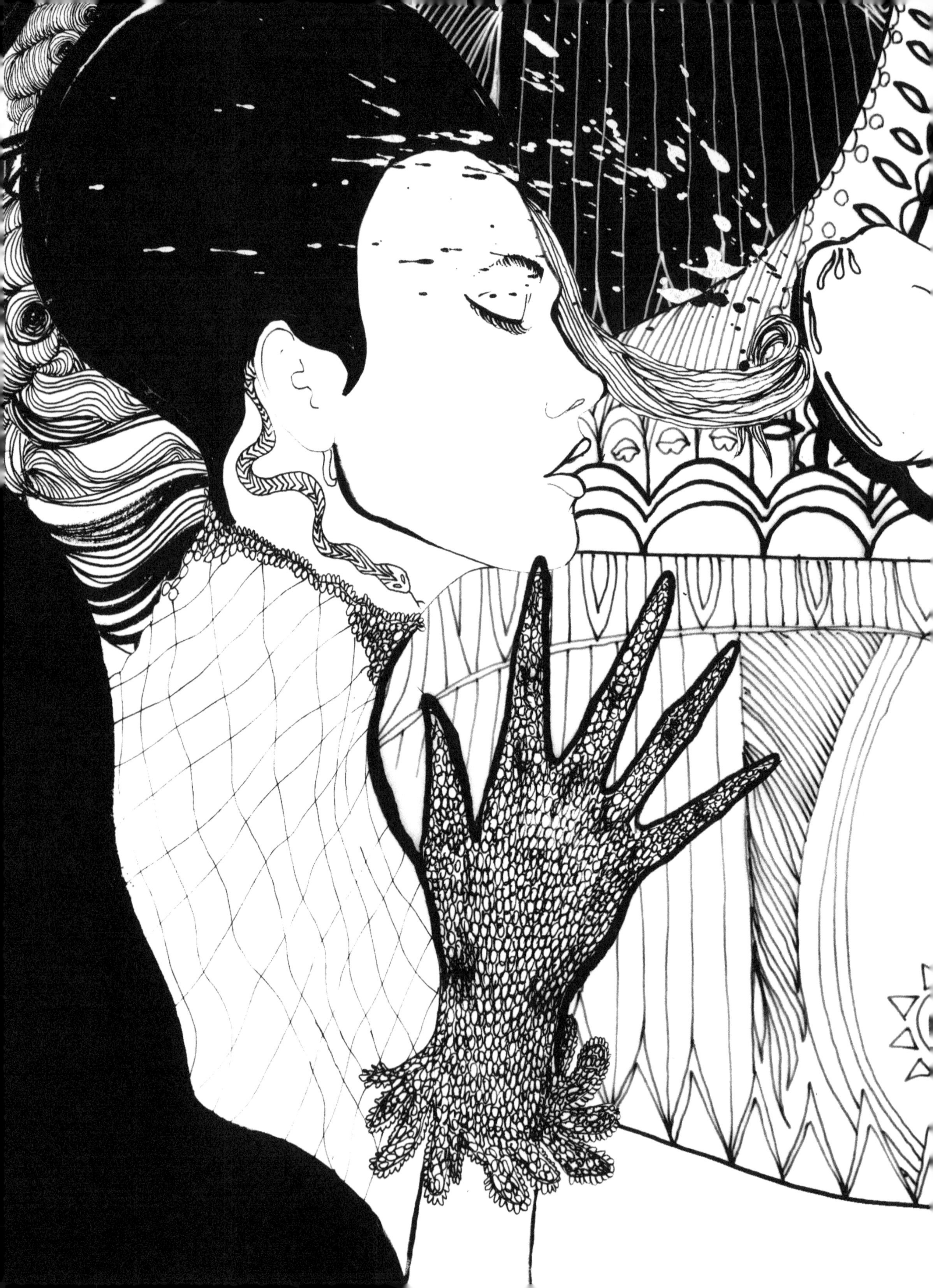

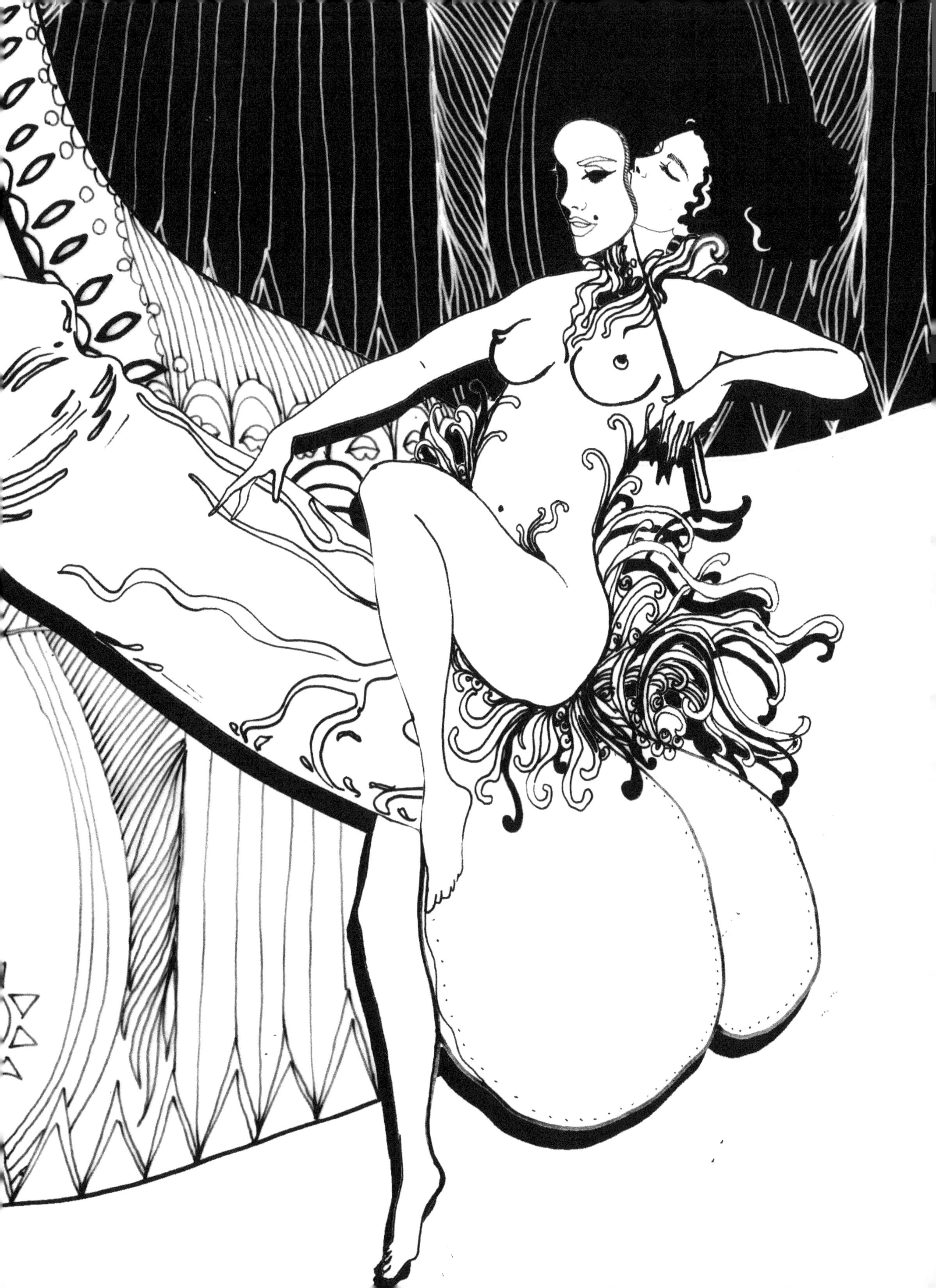

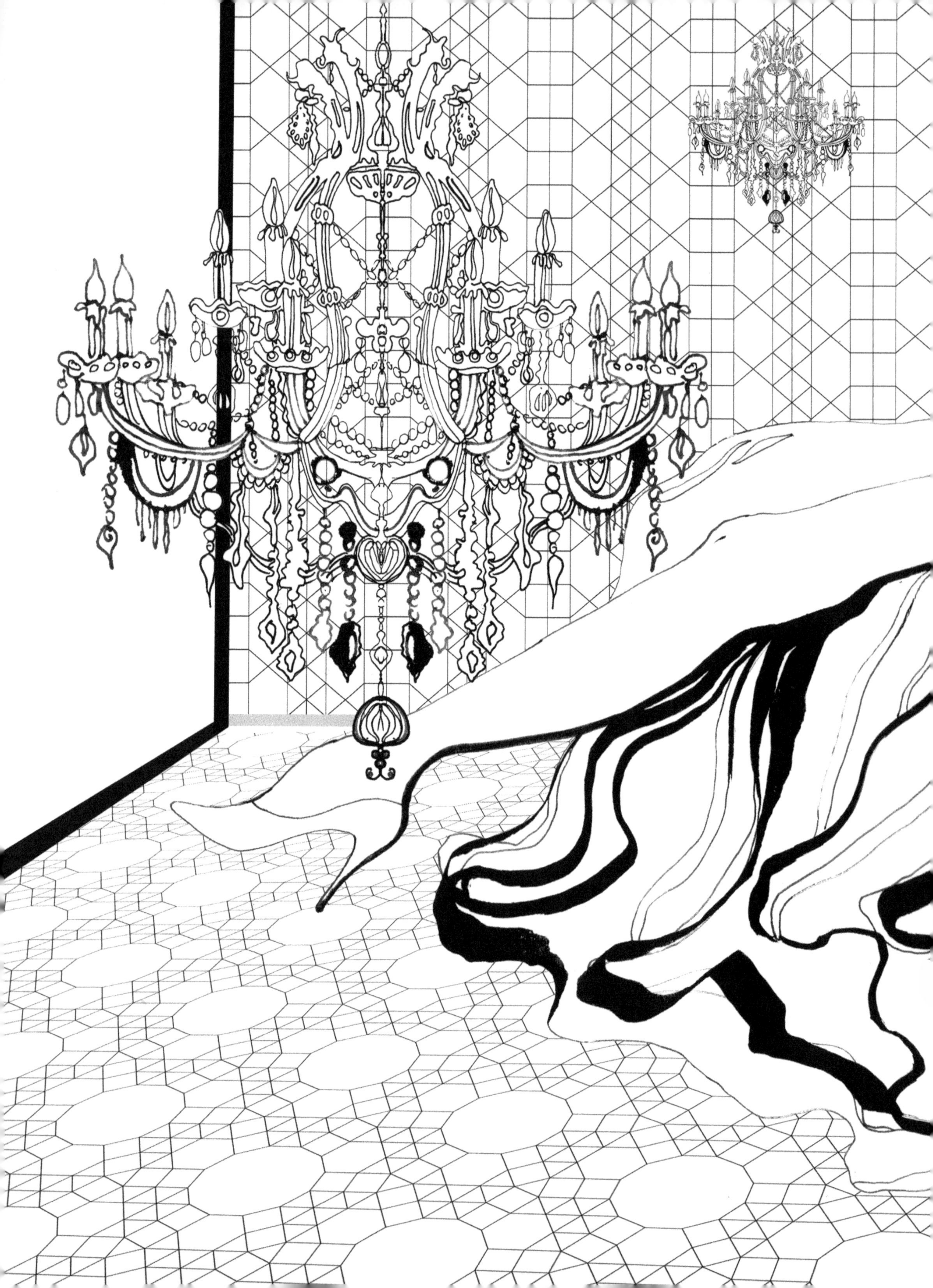

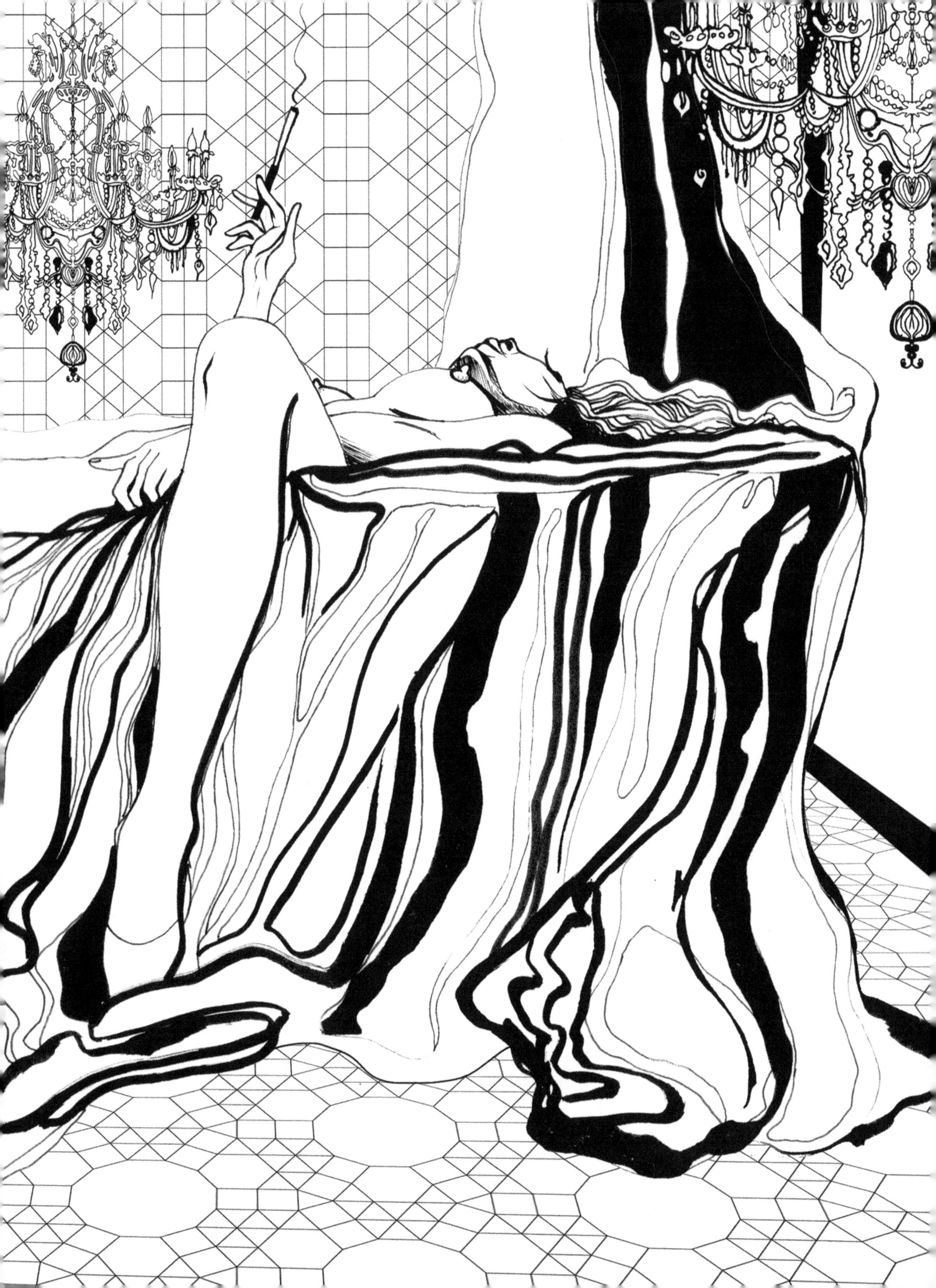

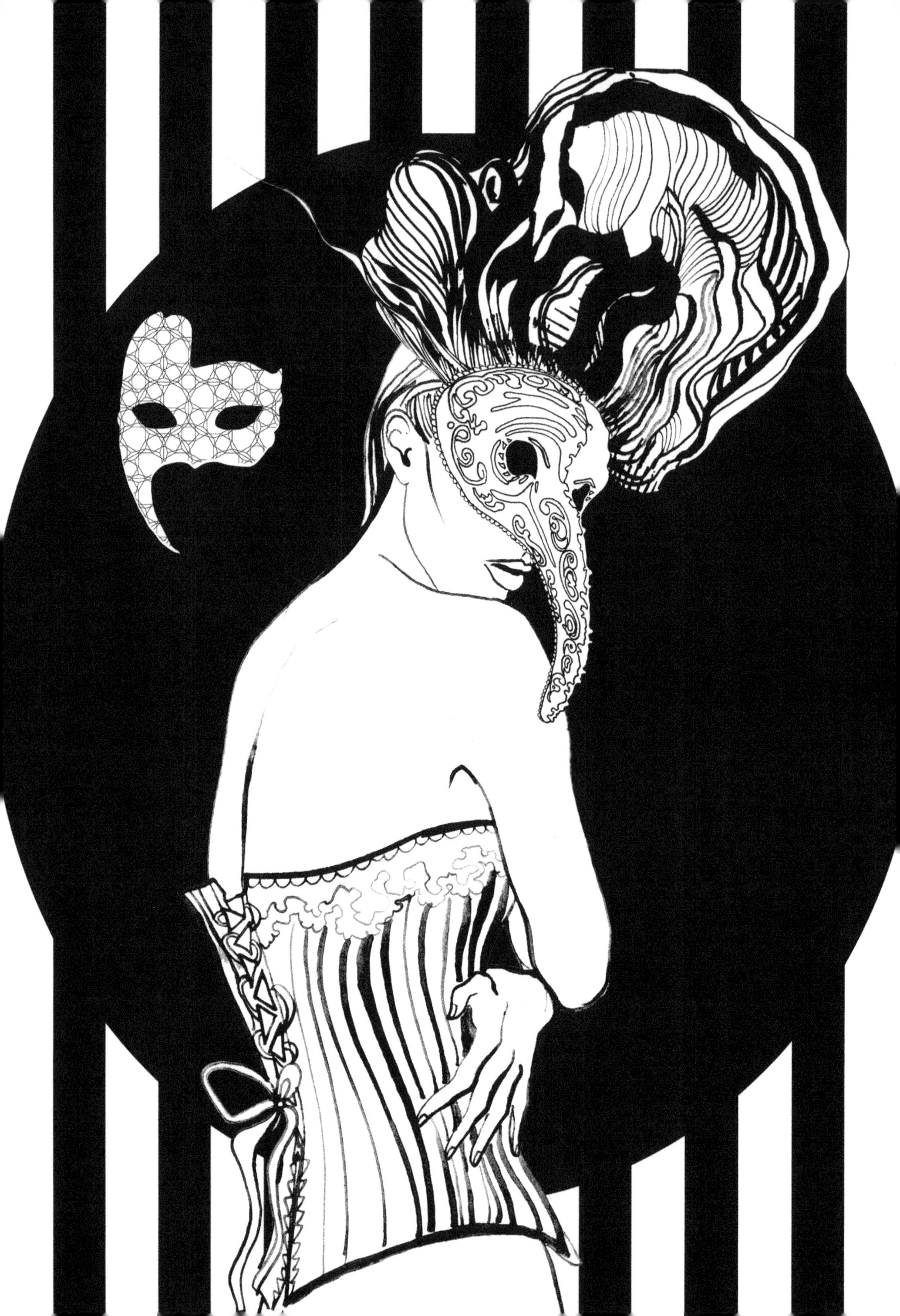

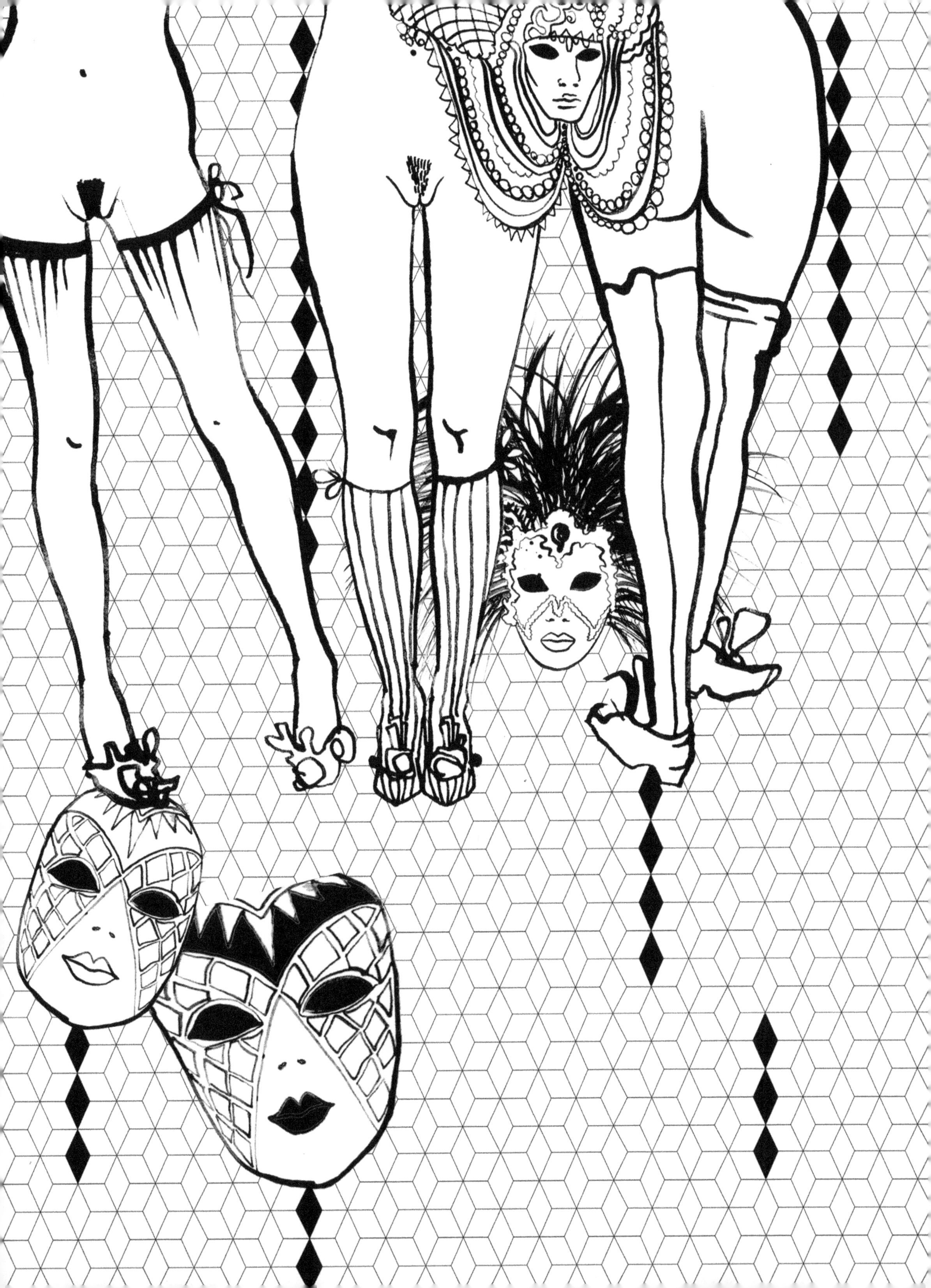

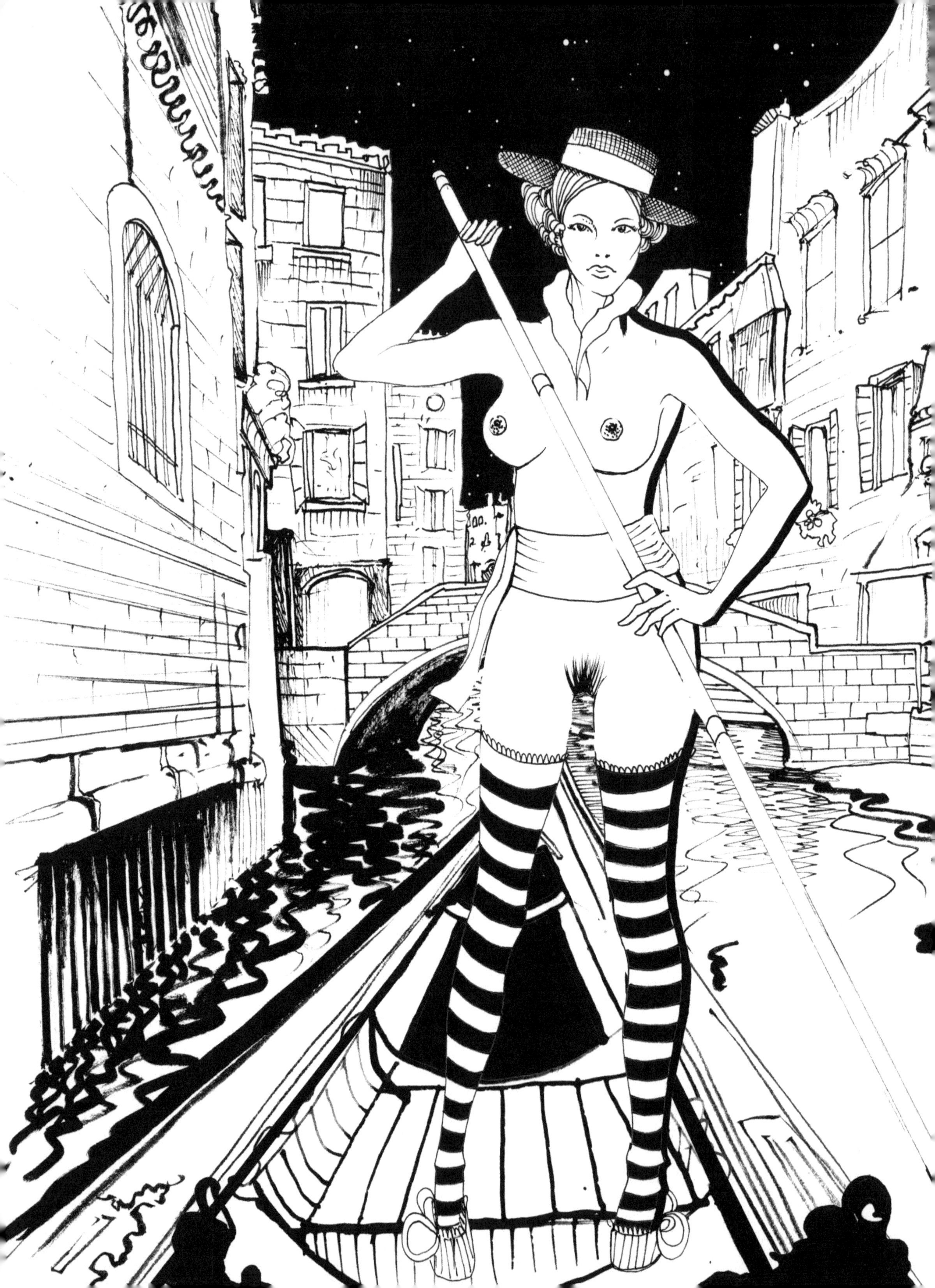

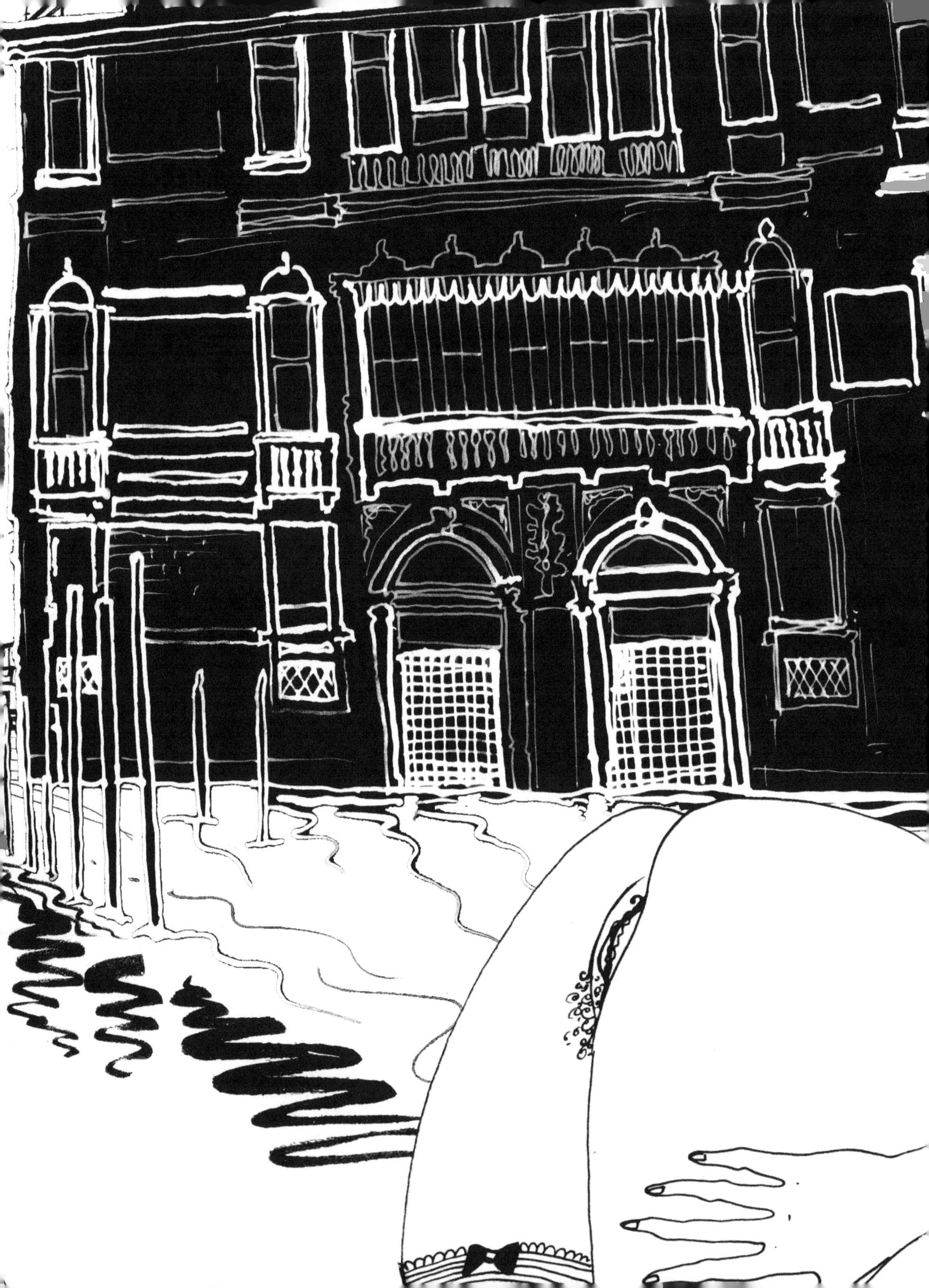

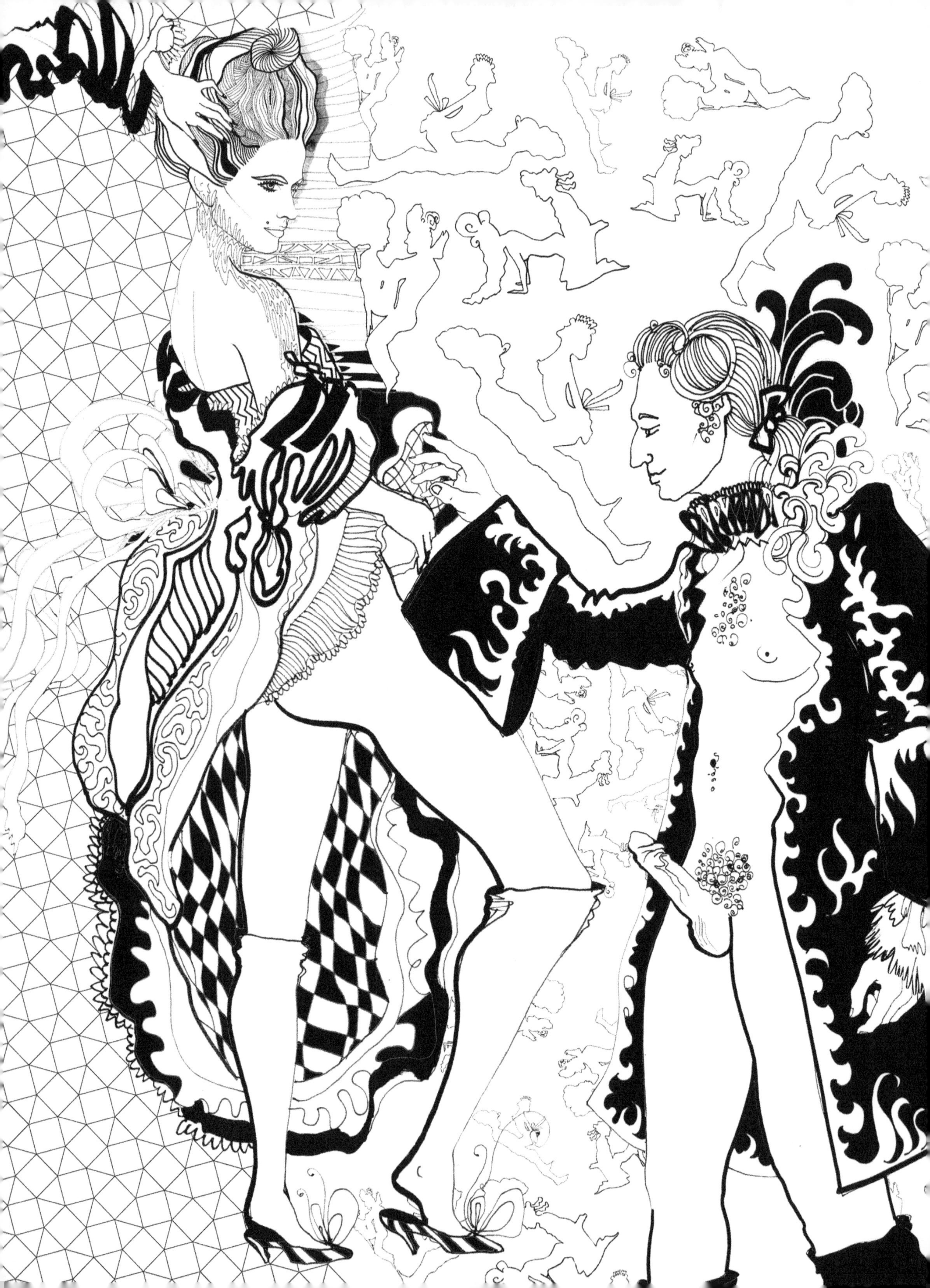

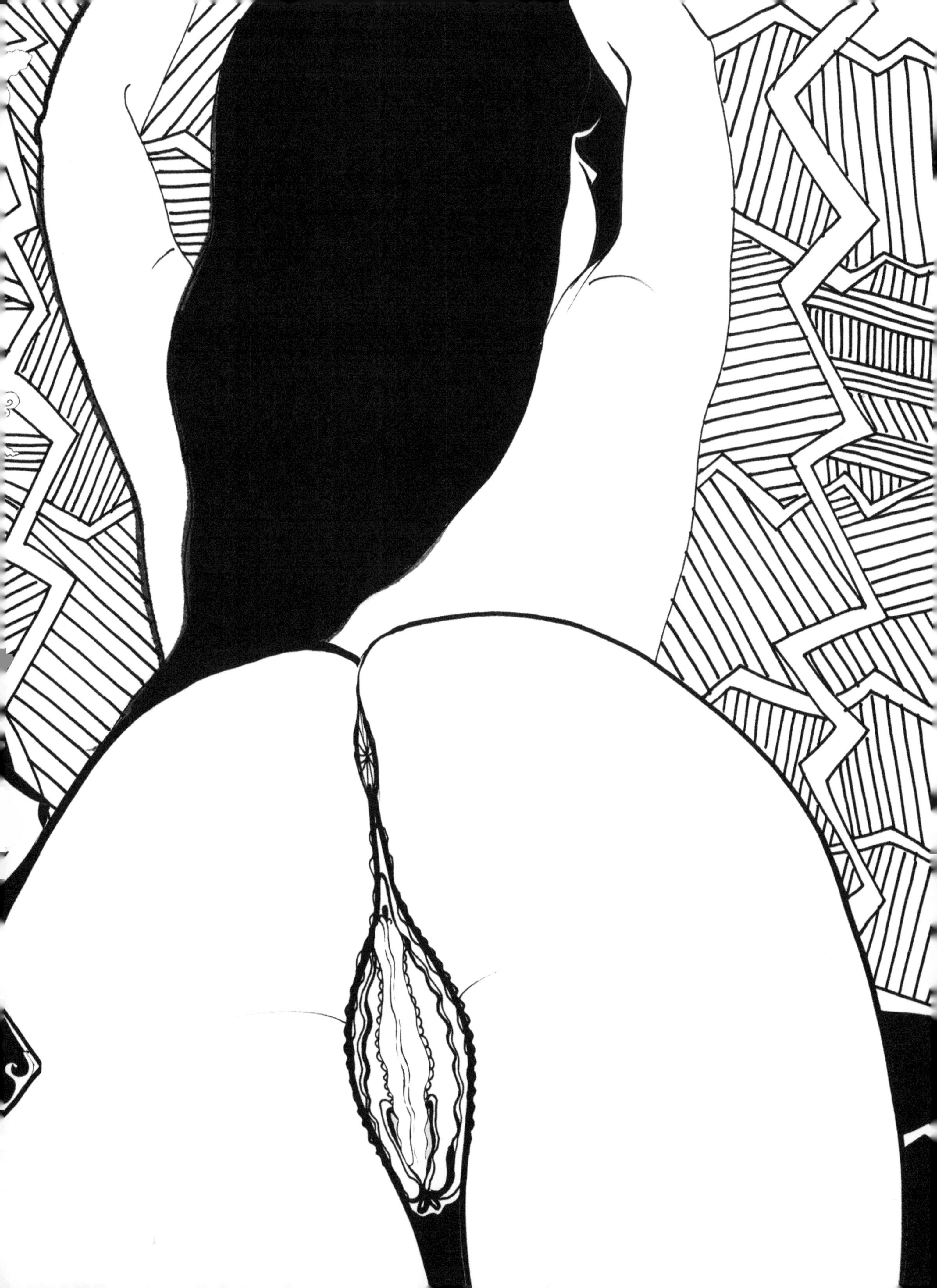

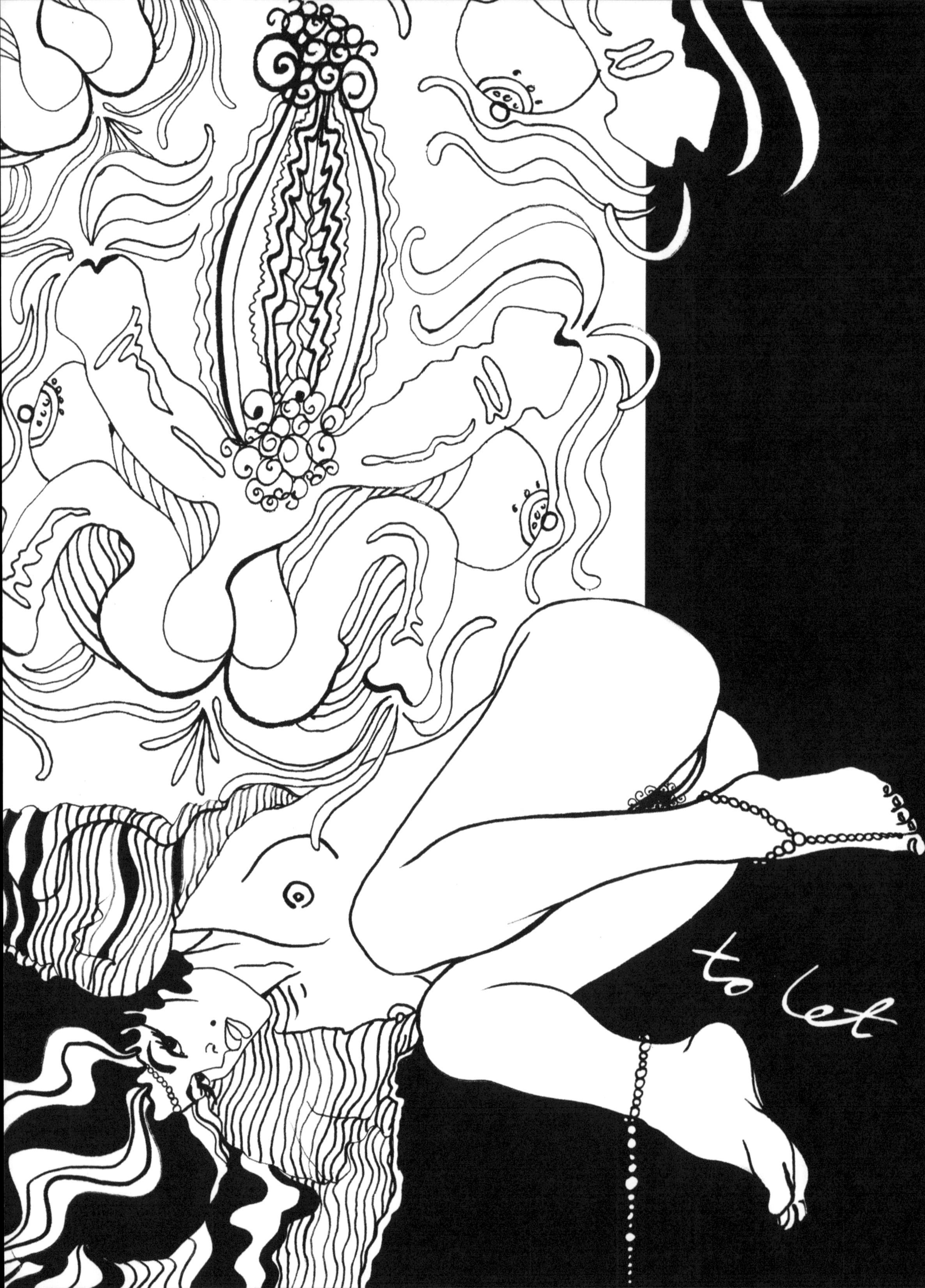
to let

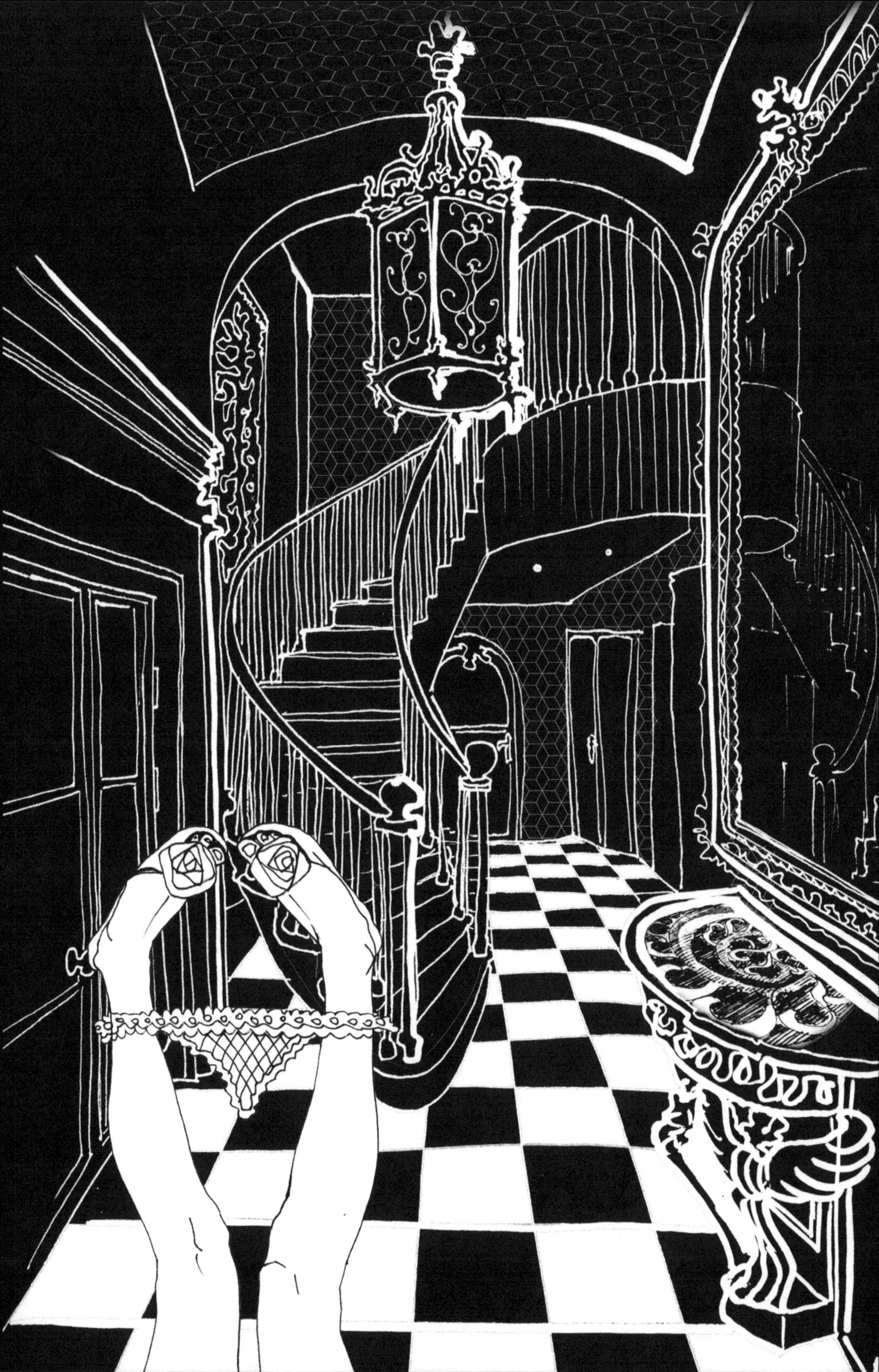

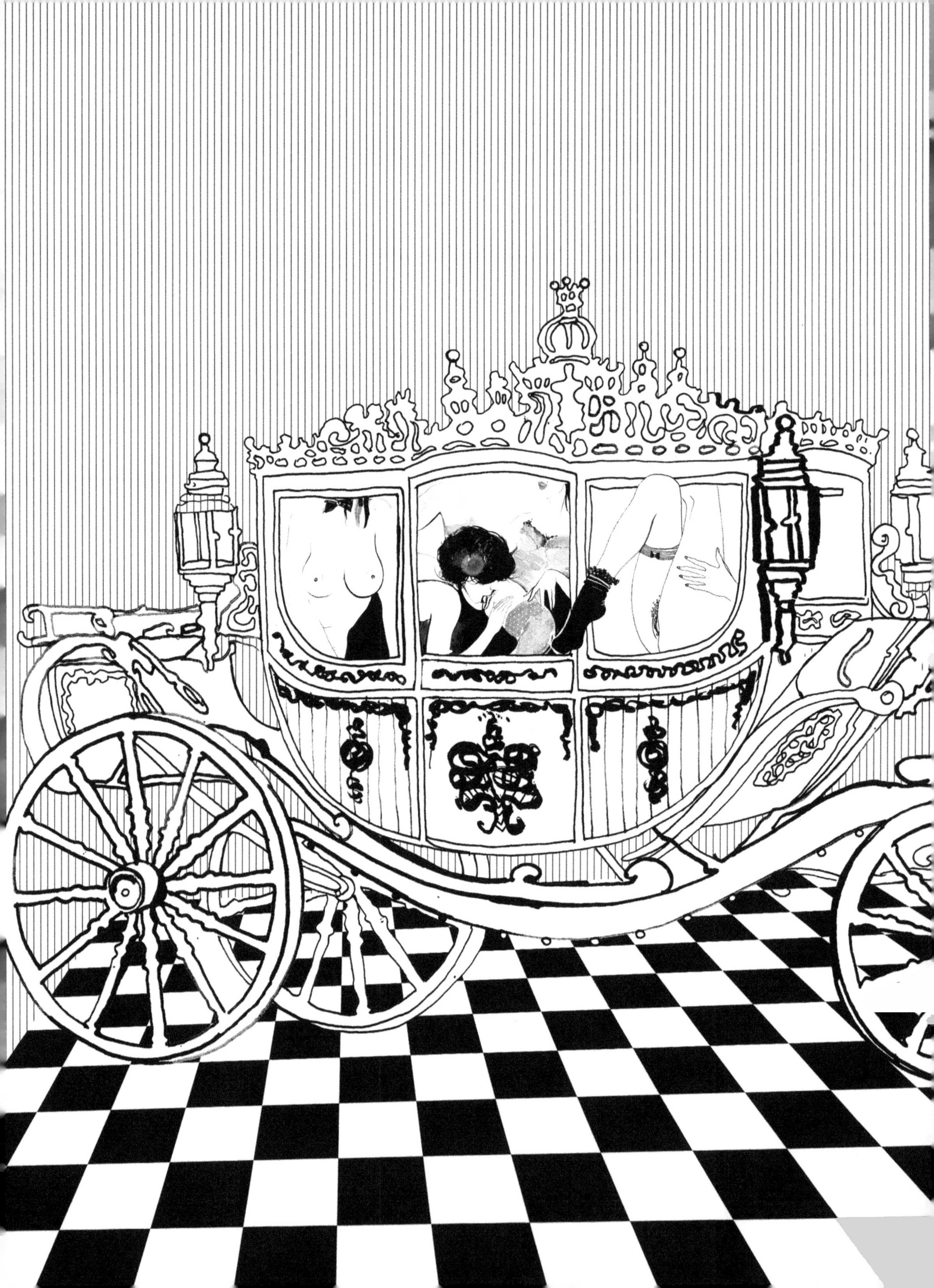

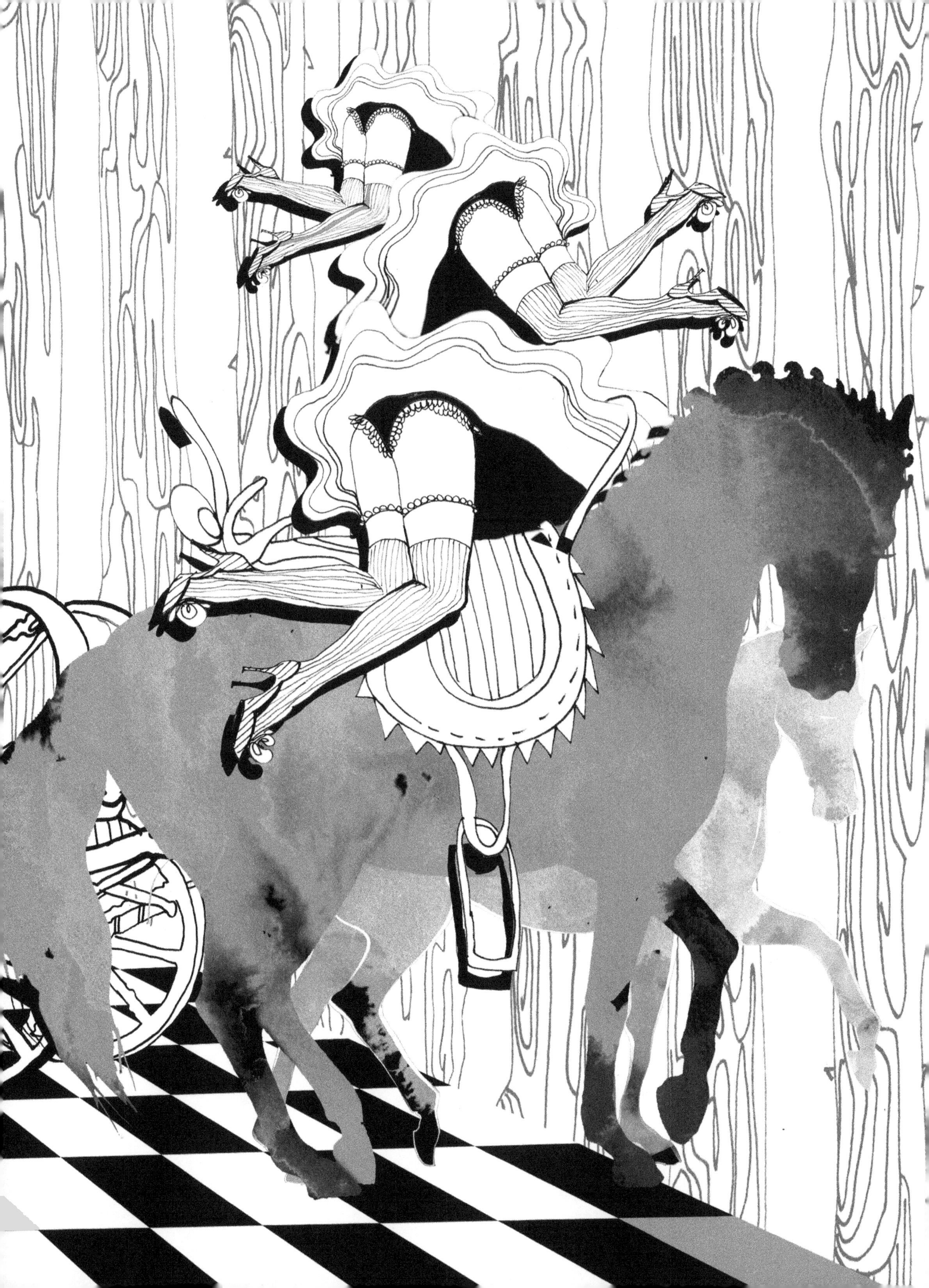

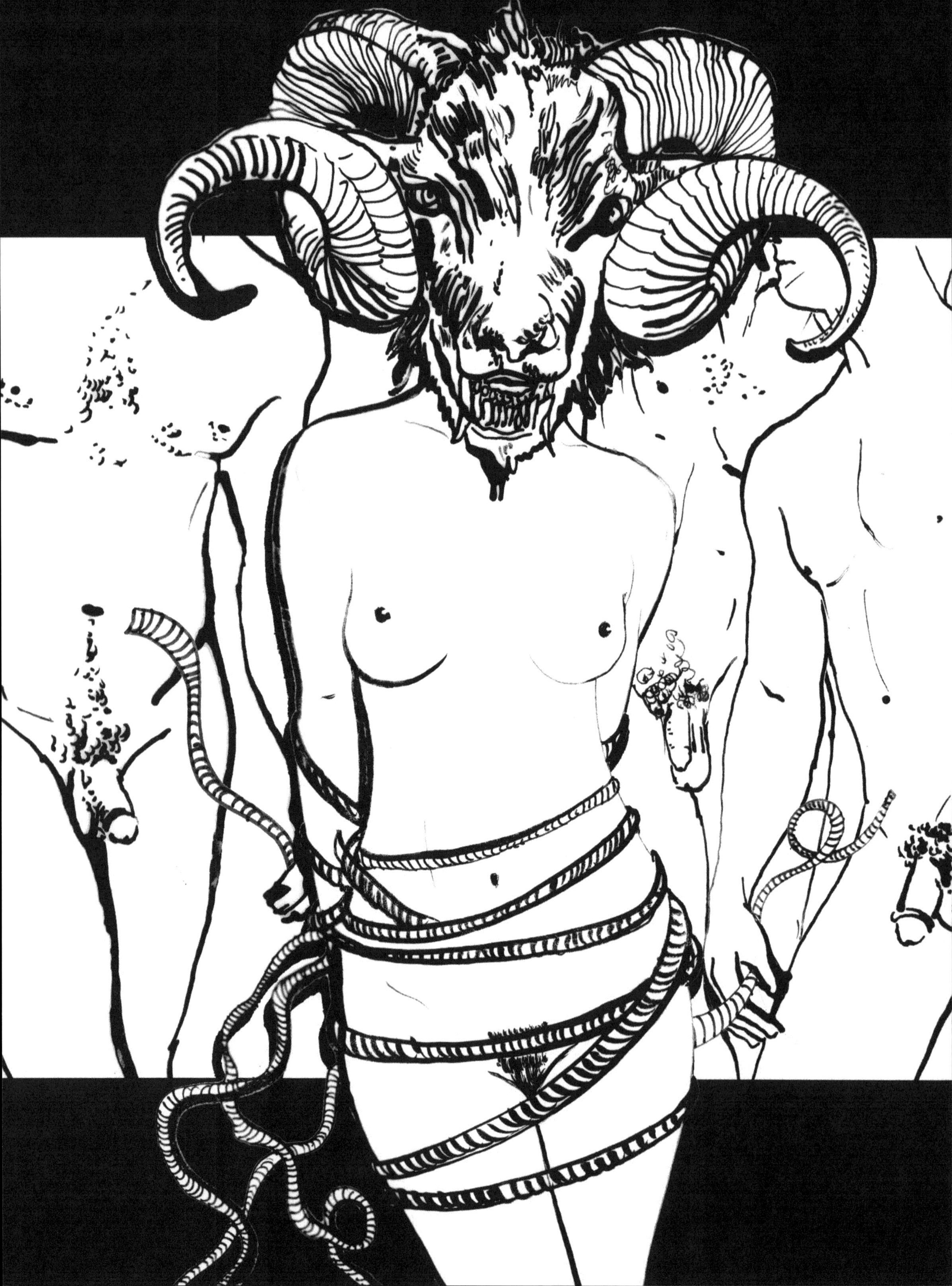

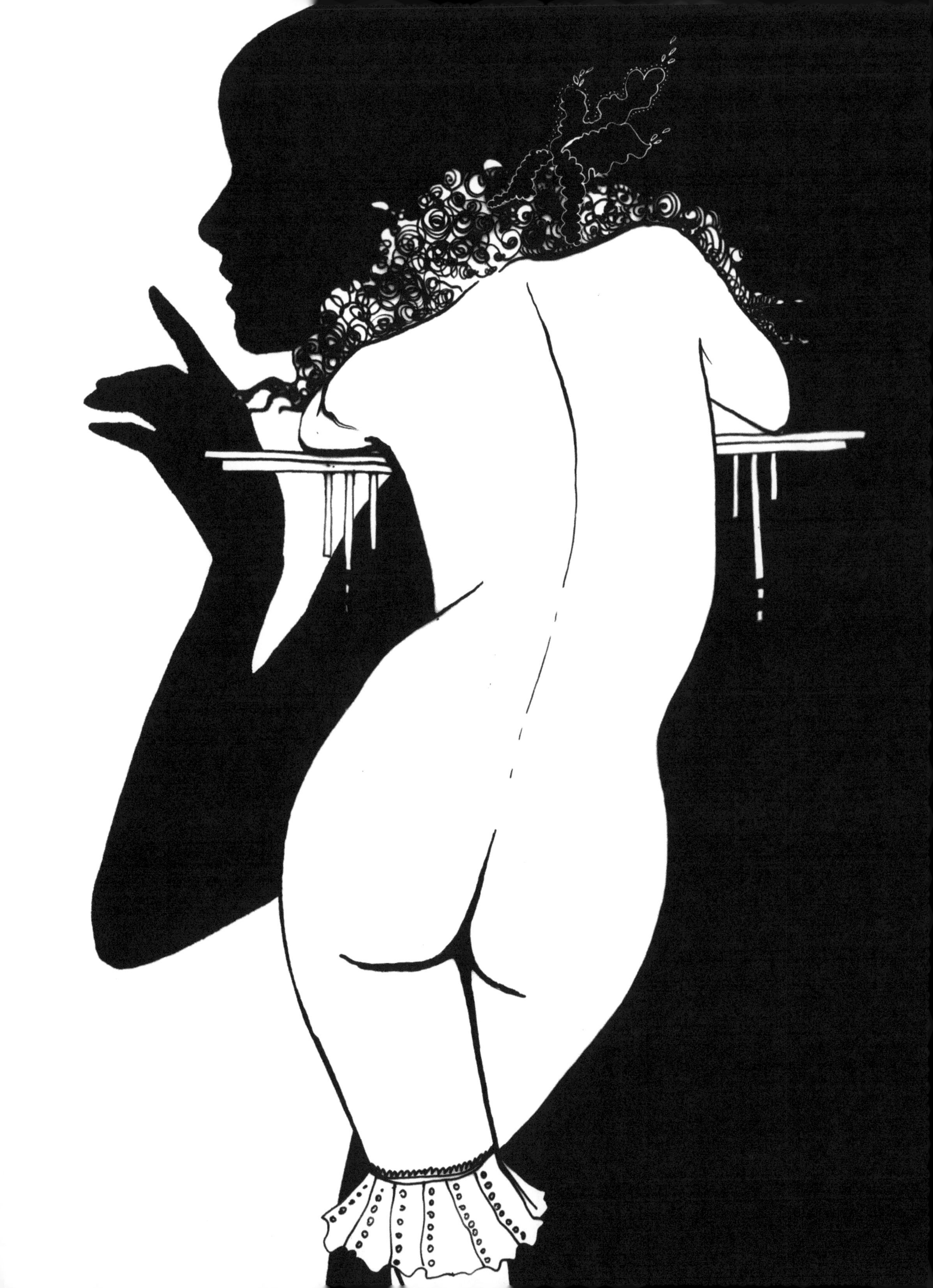

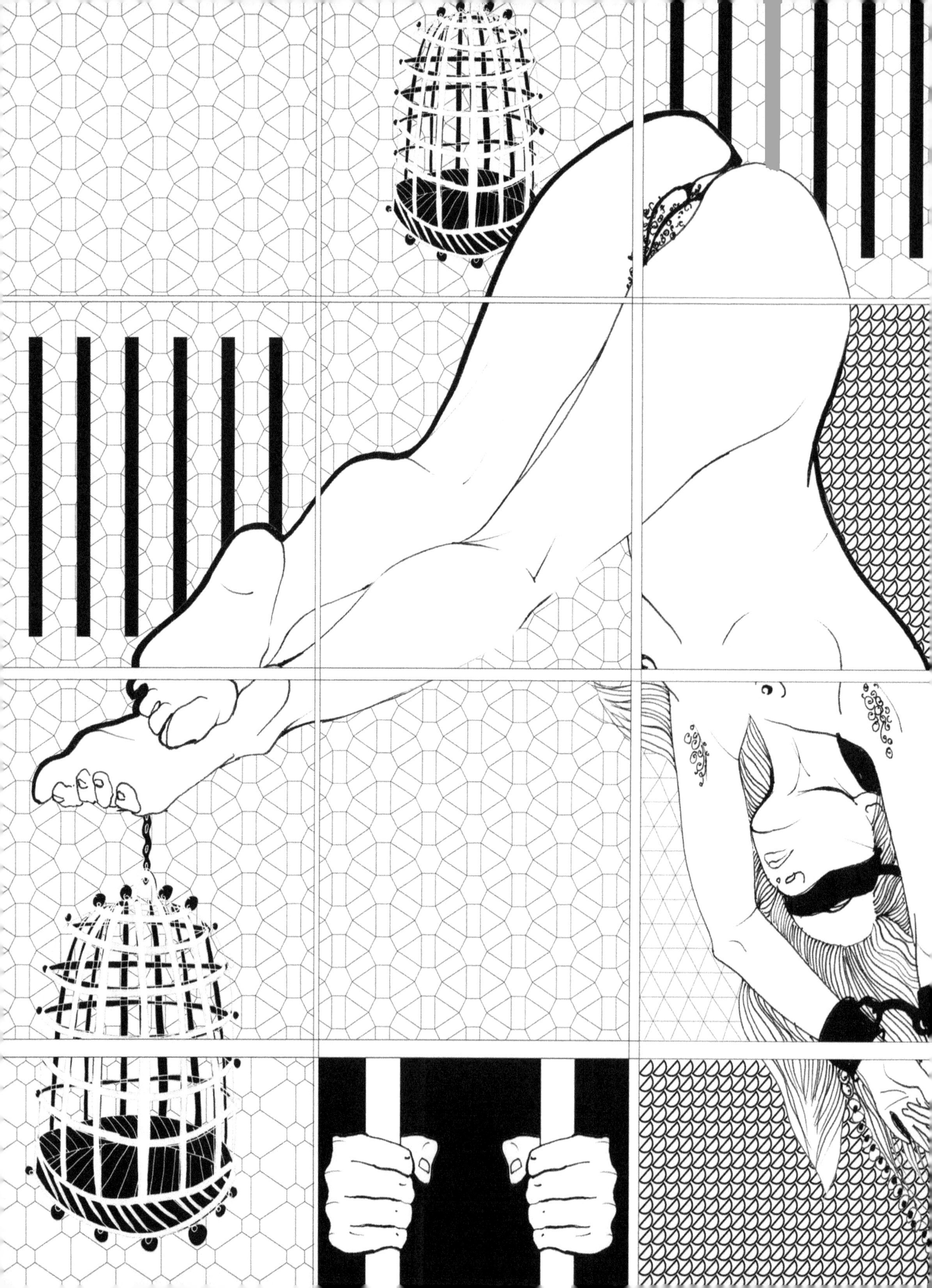

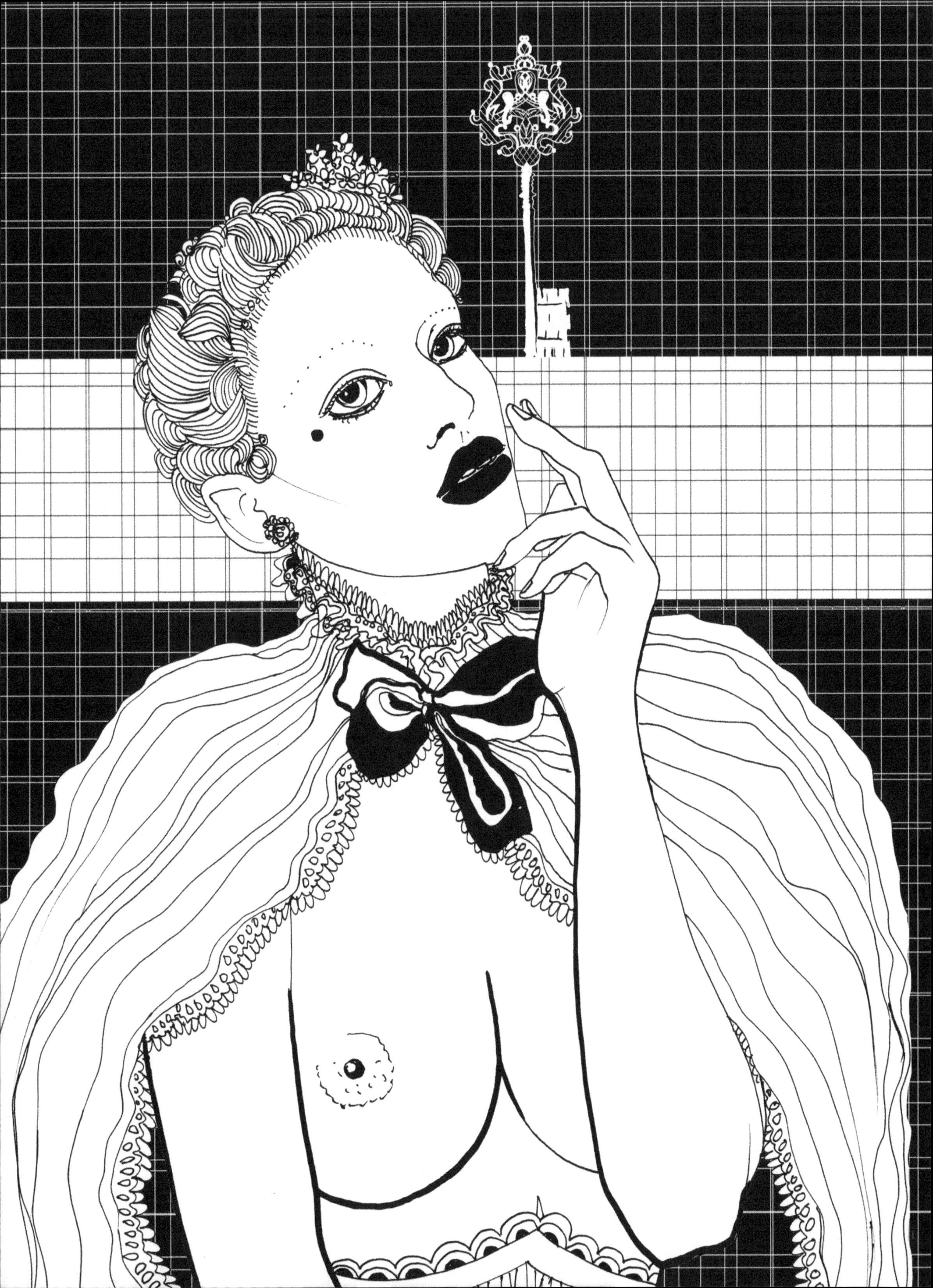

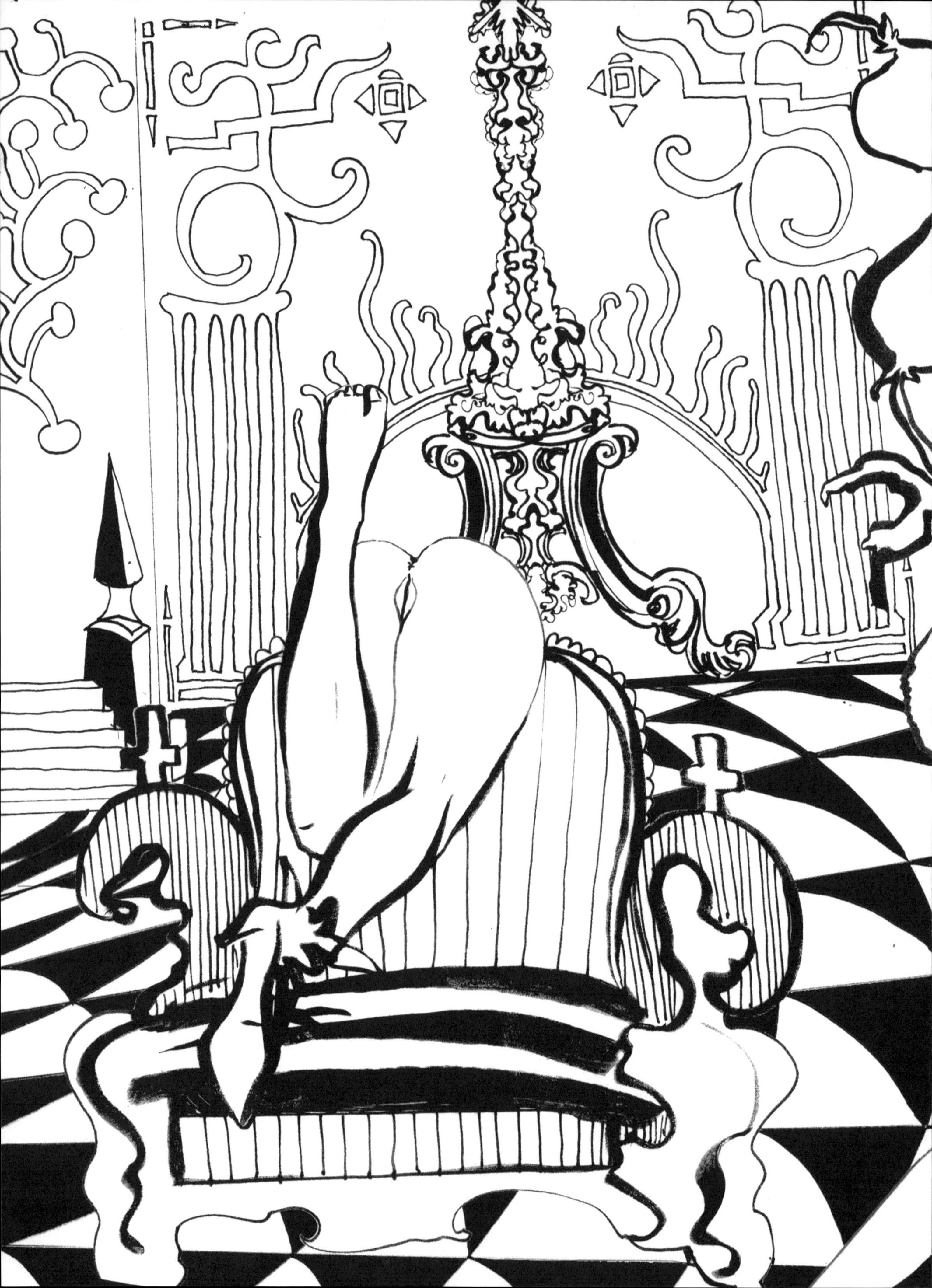

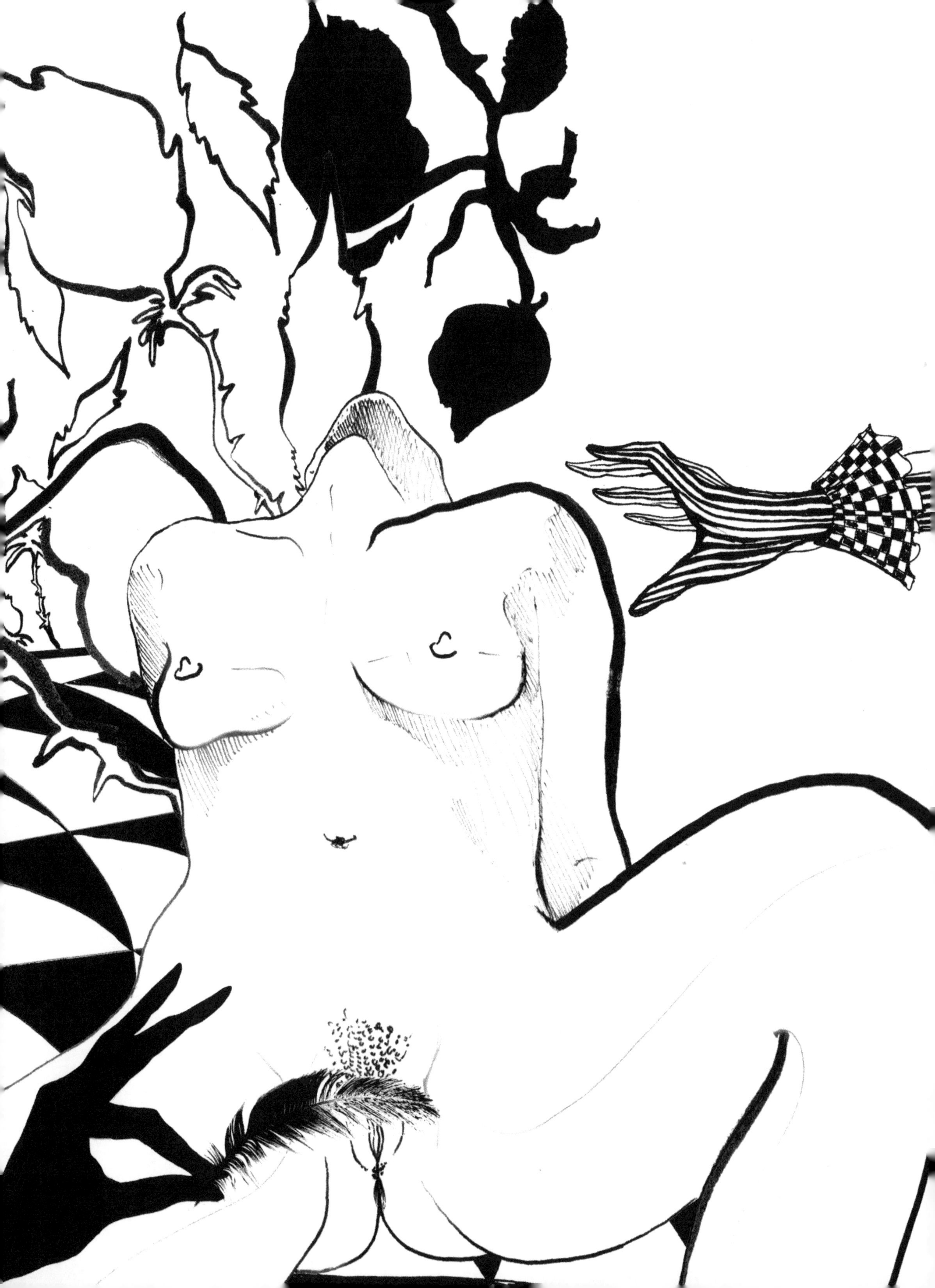

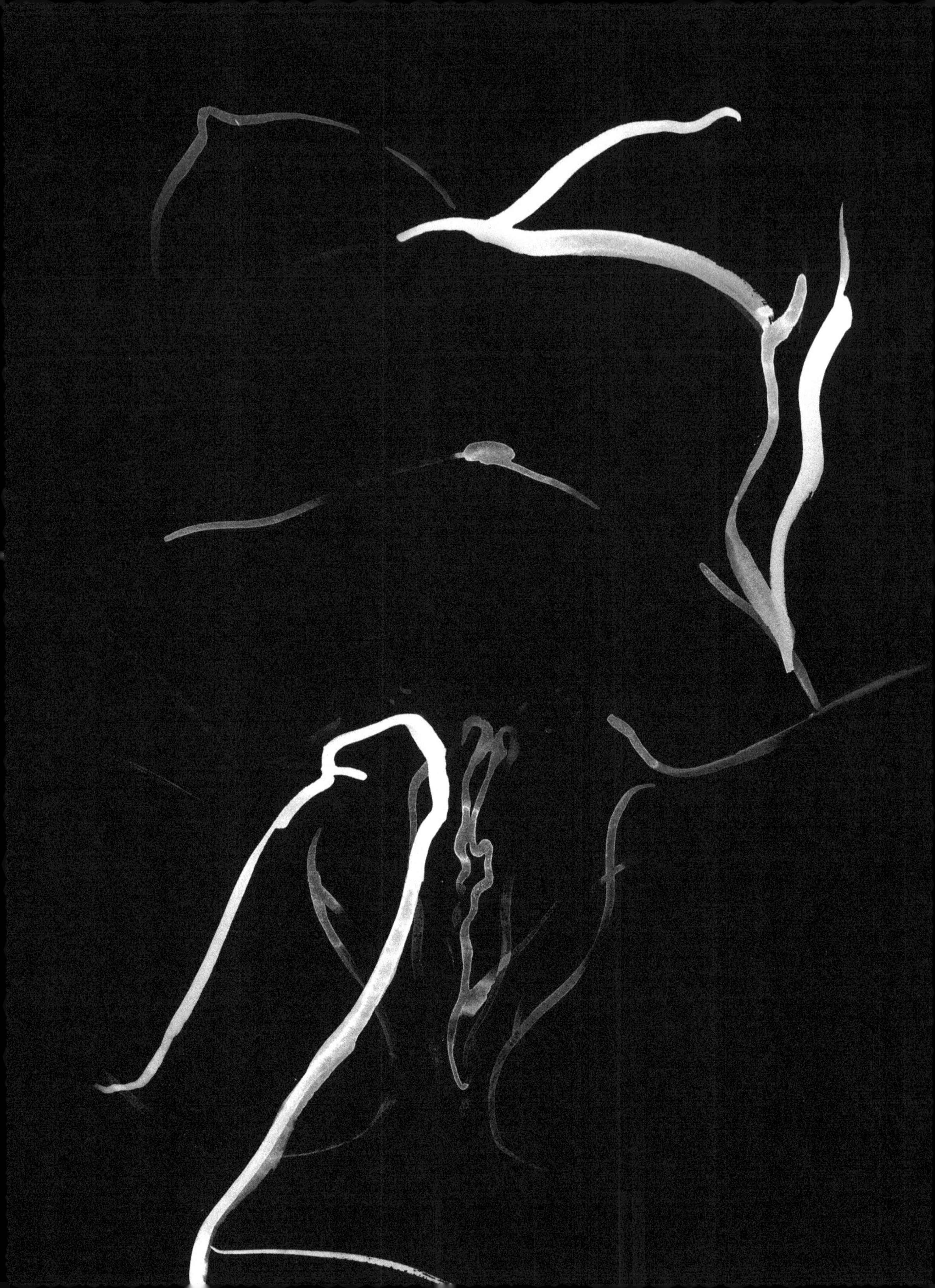

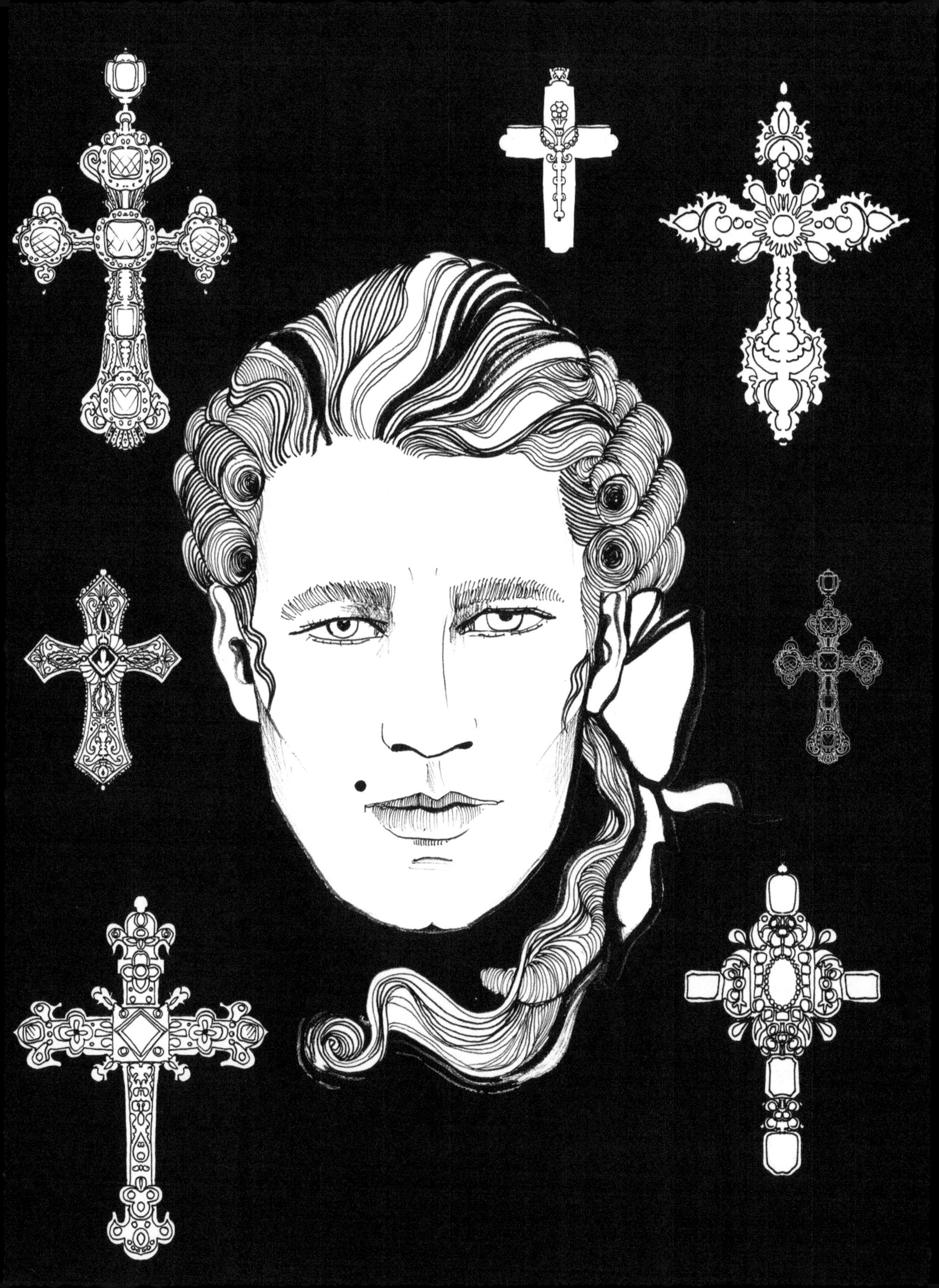

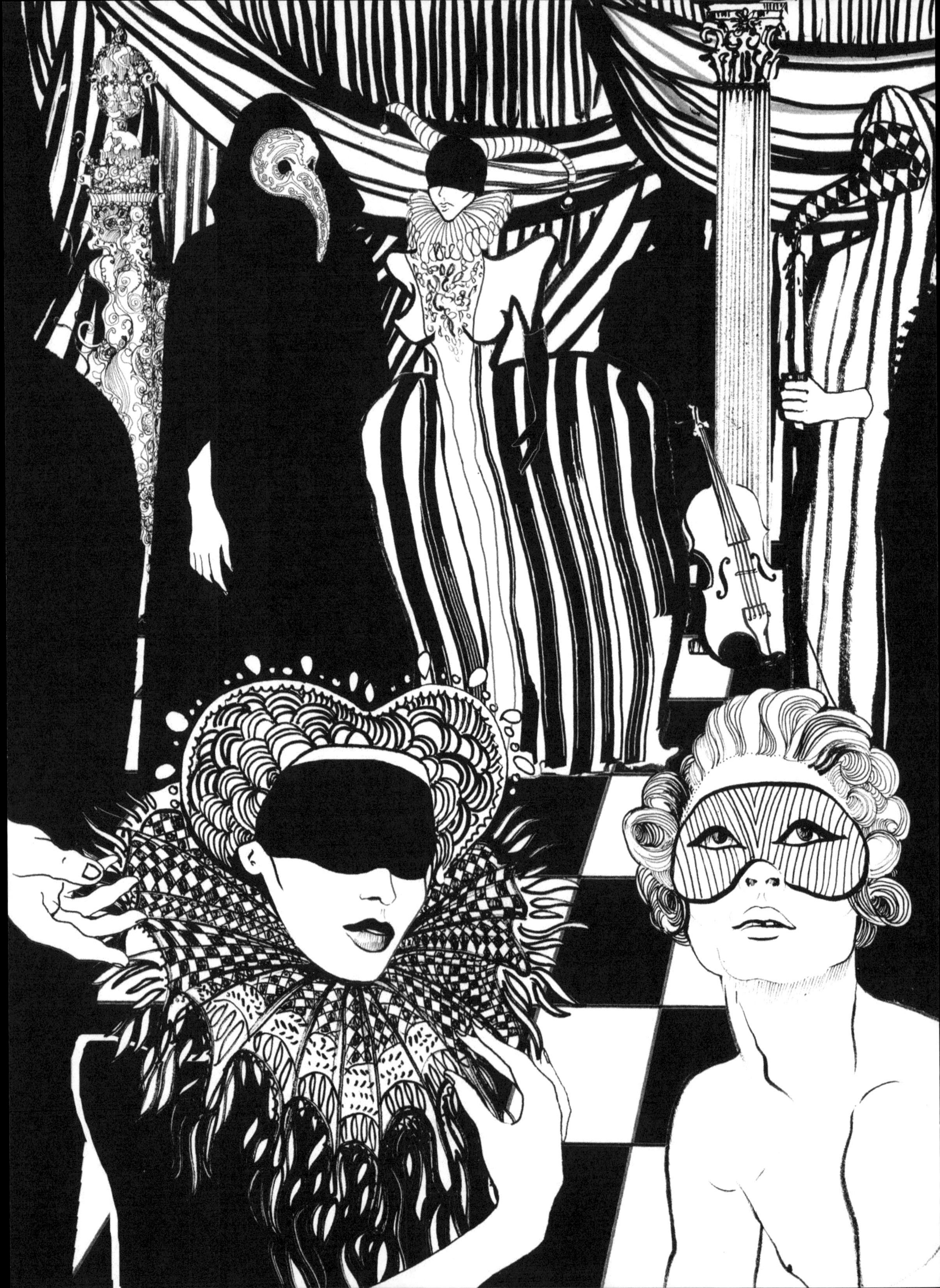

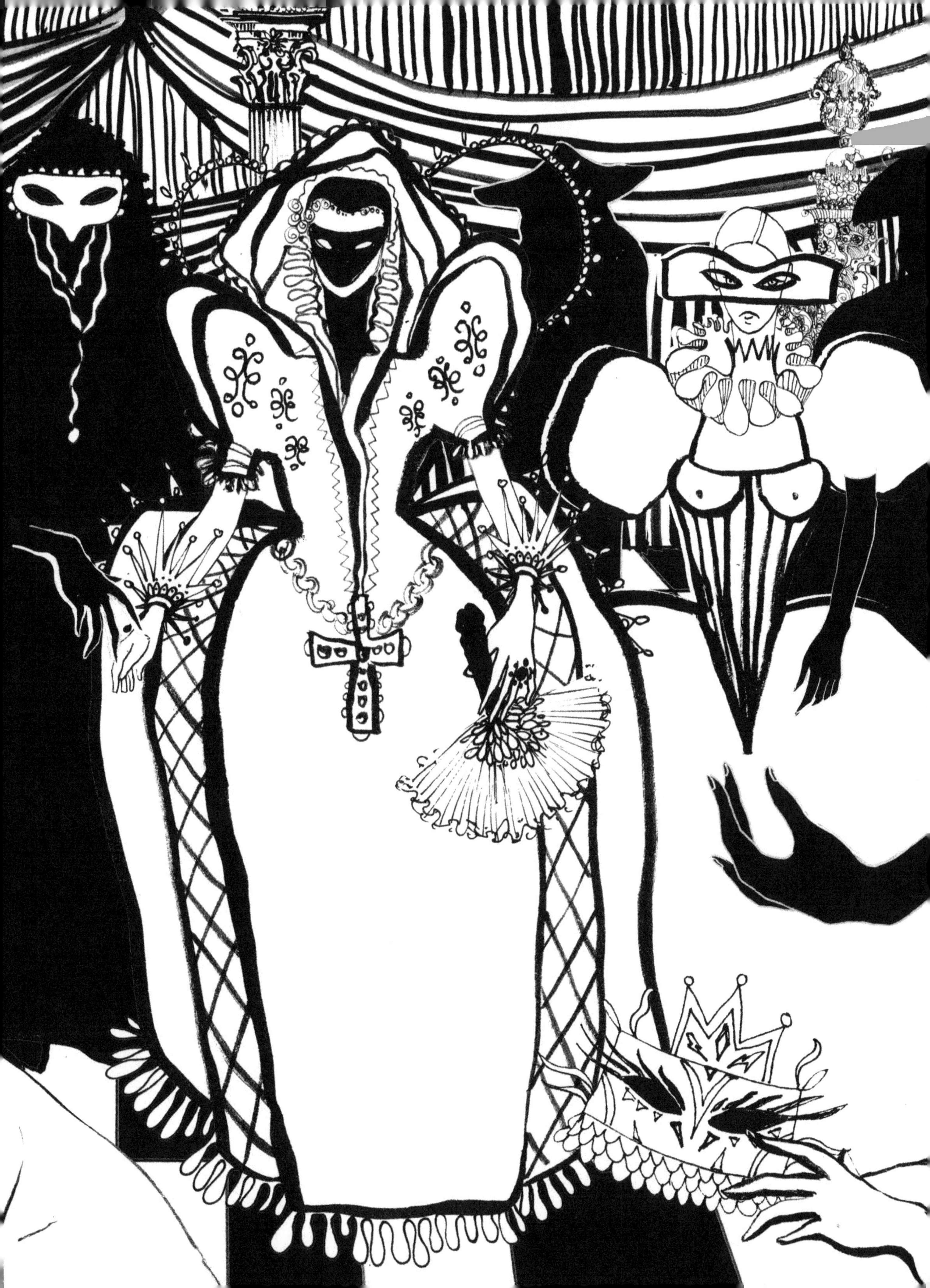

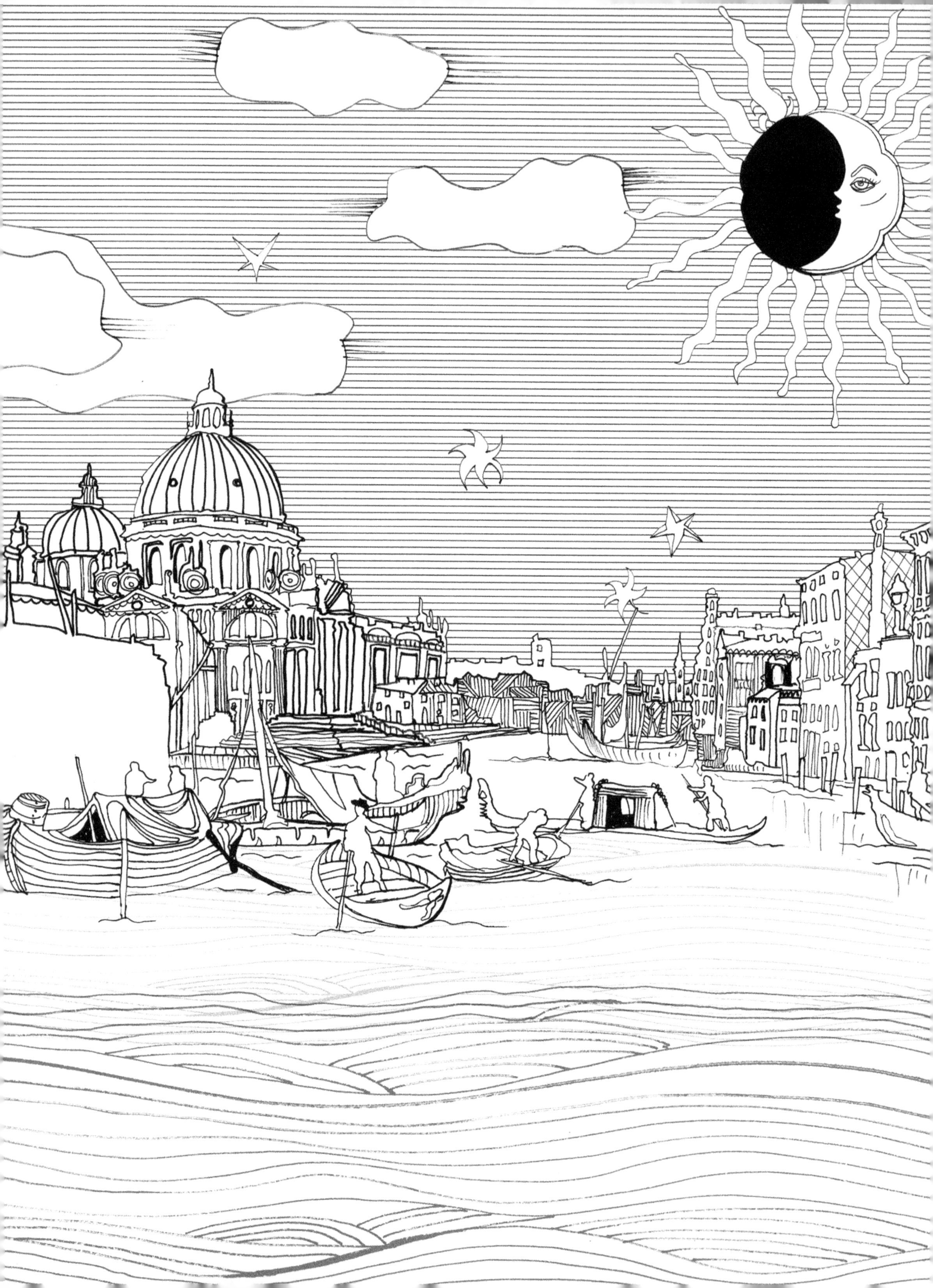

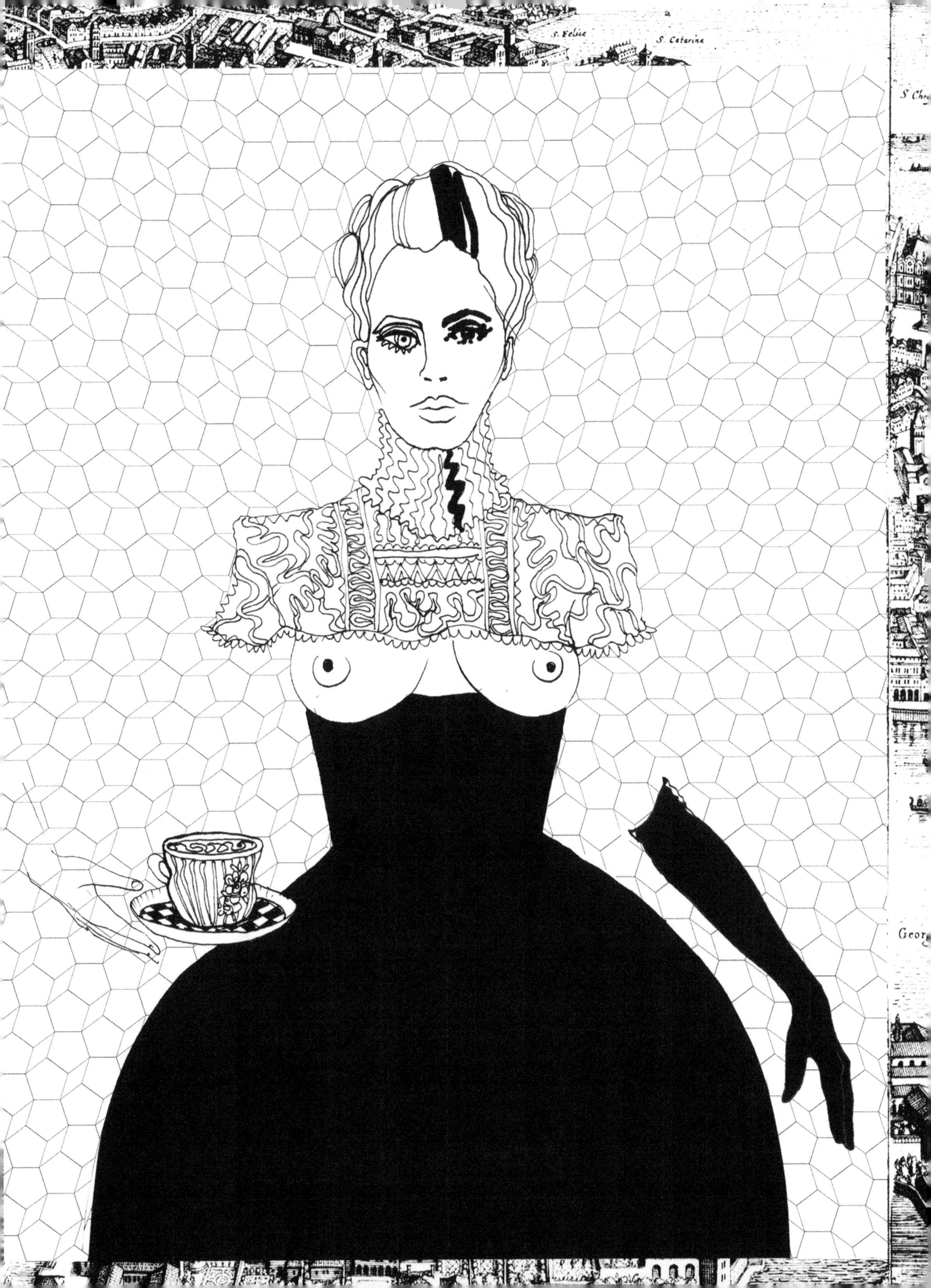
S. Felice
S. Catarina

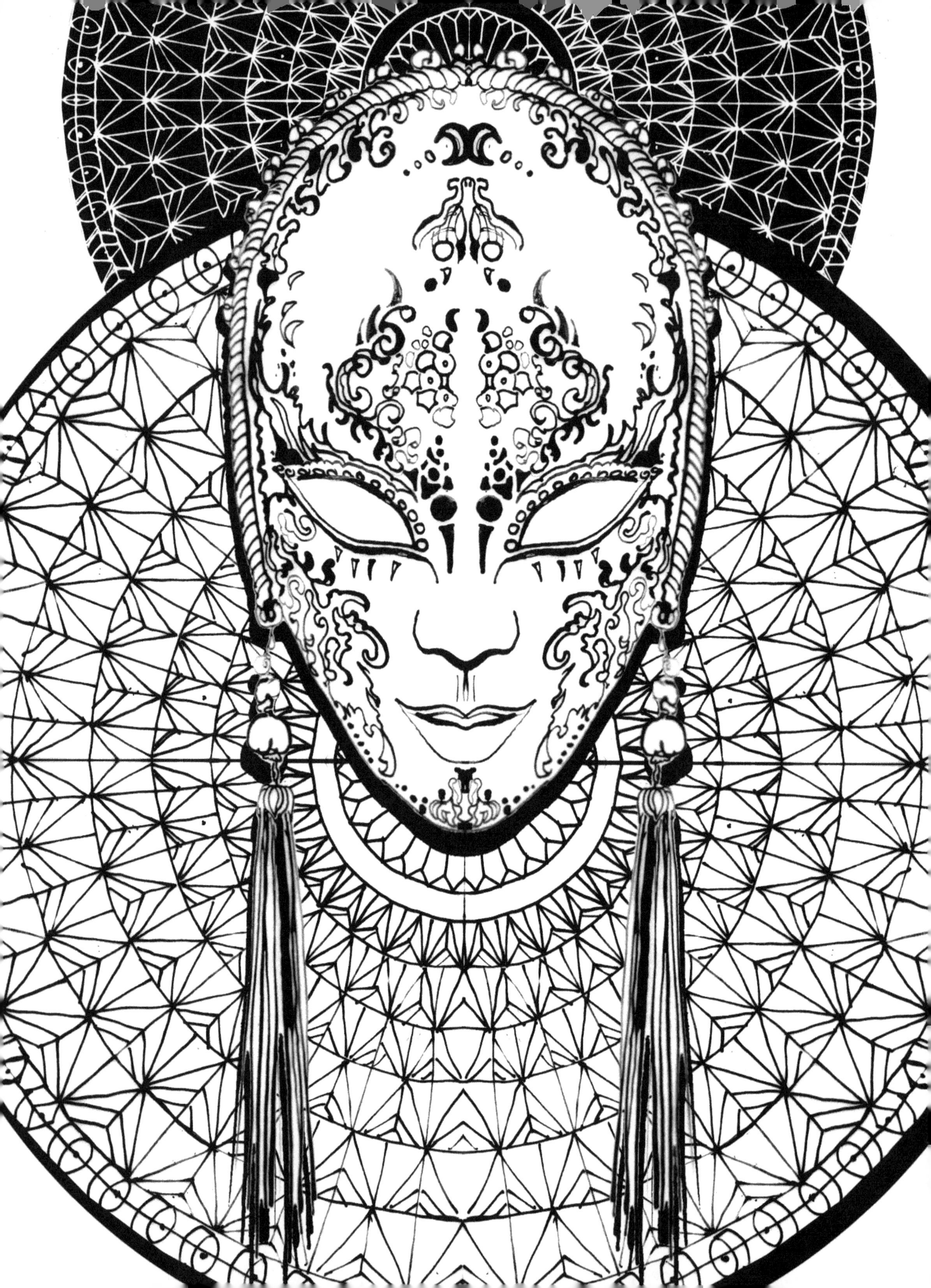

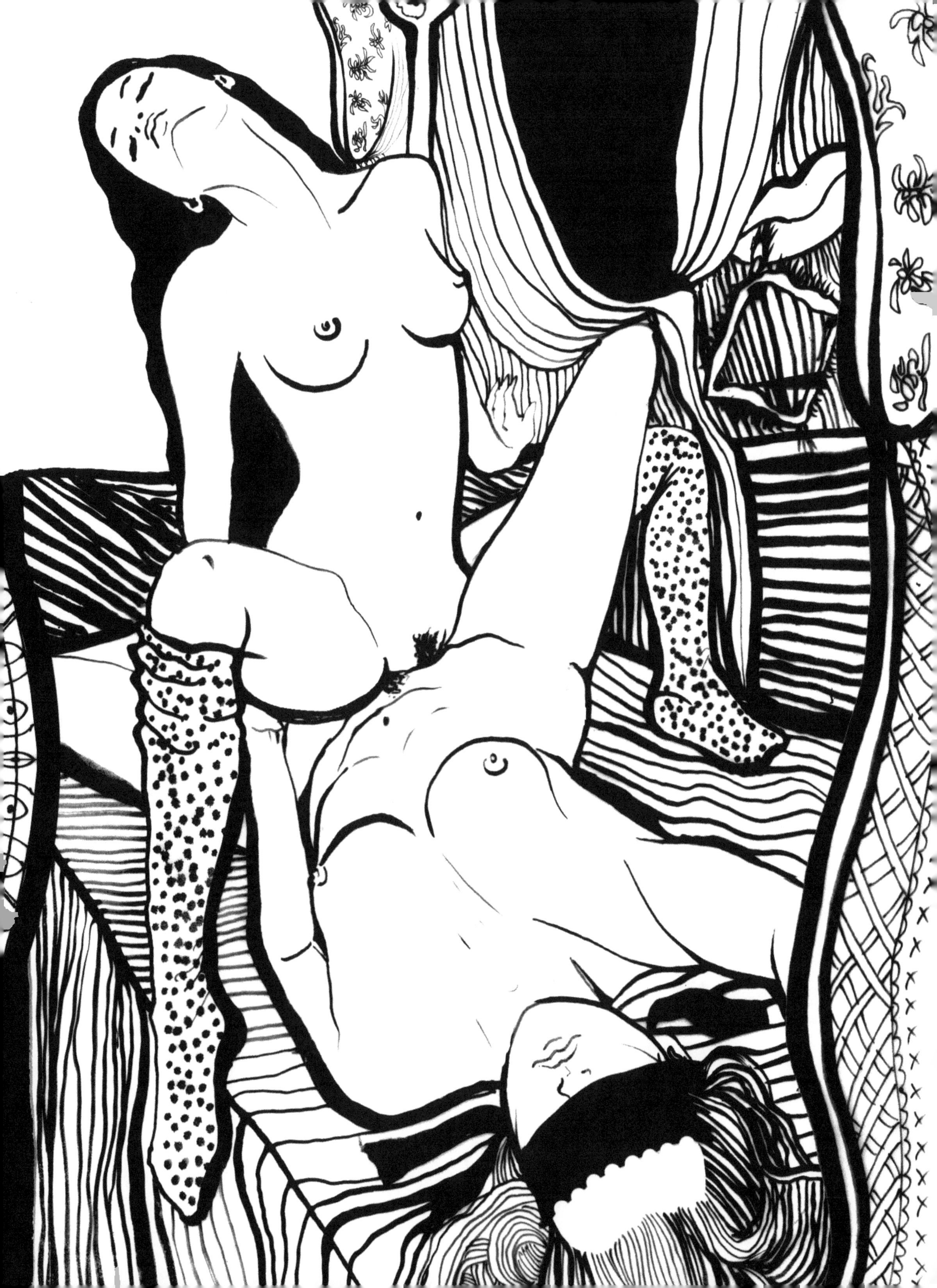

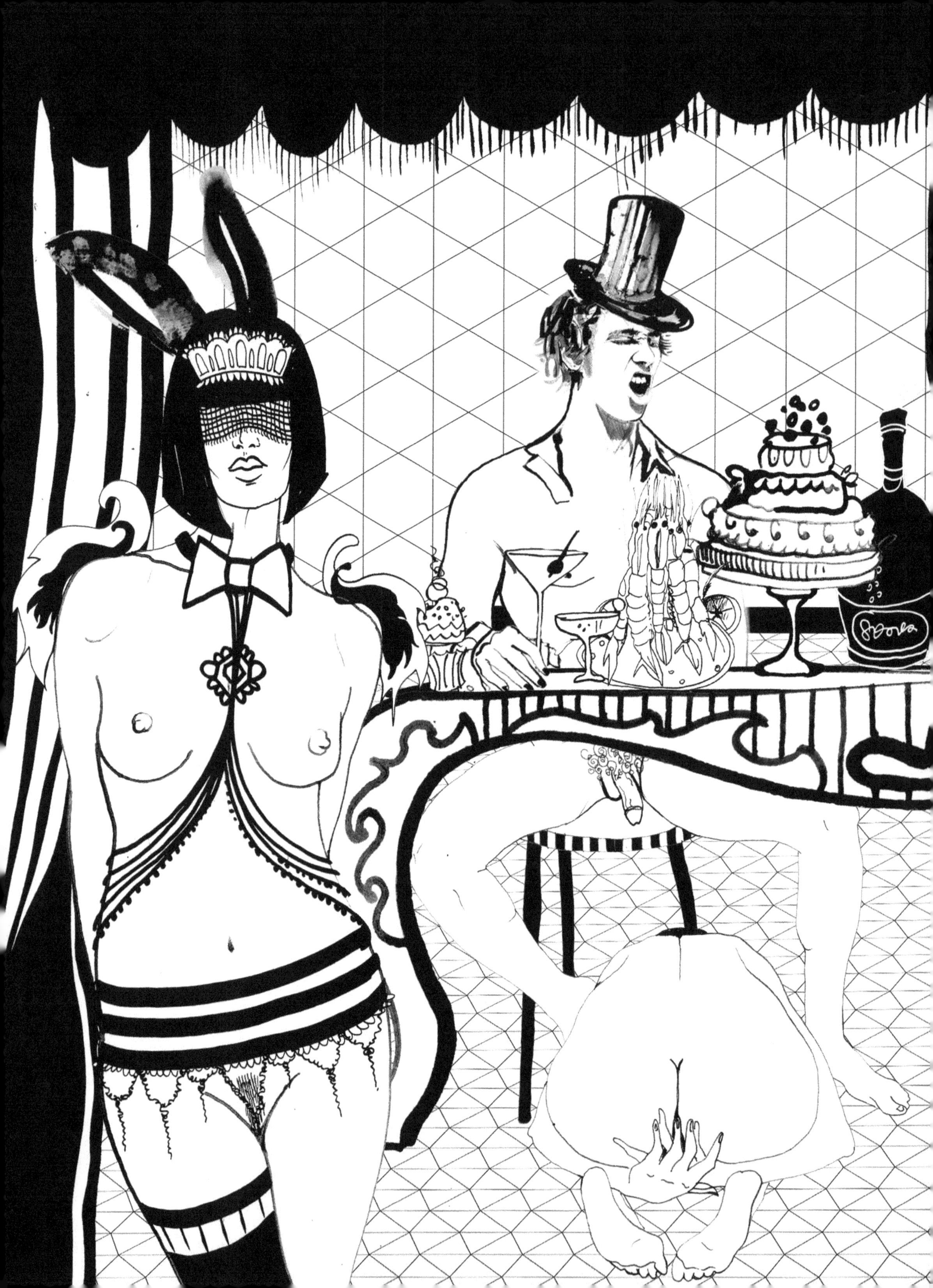

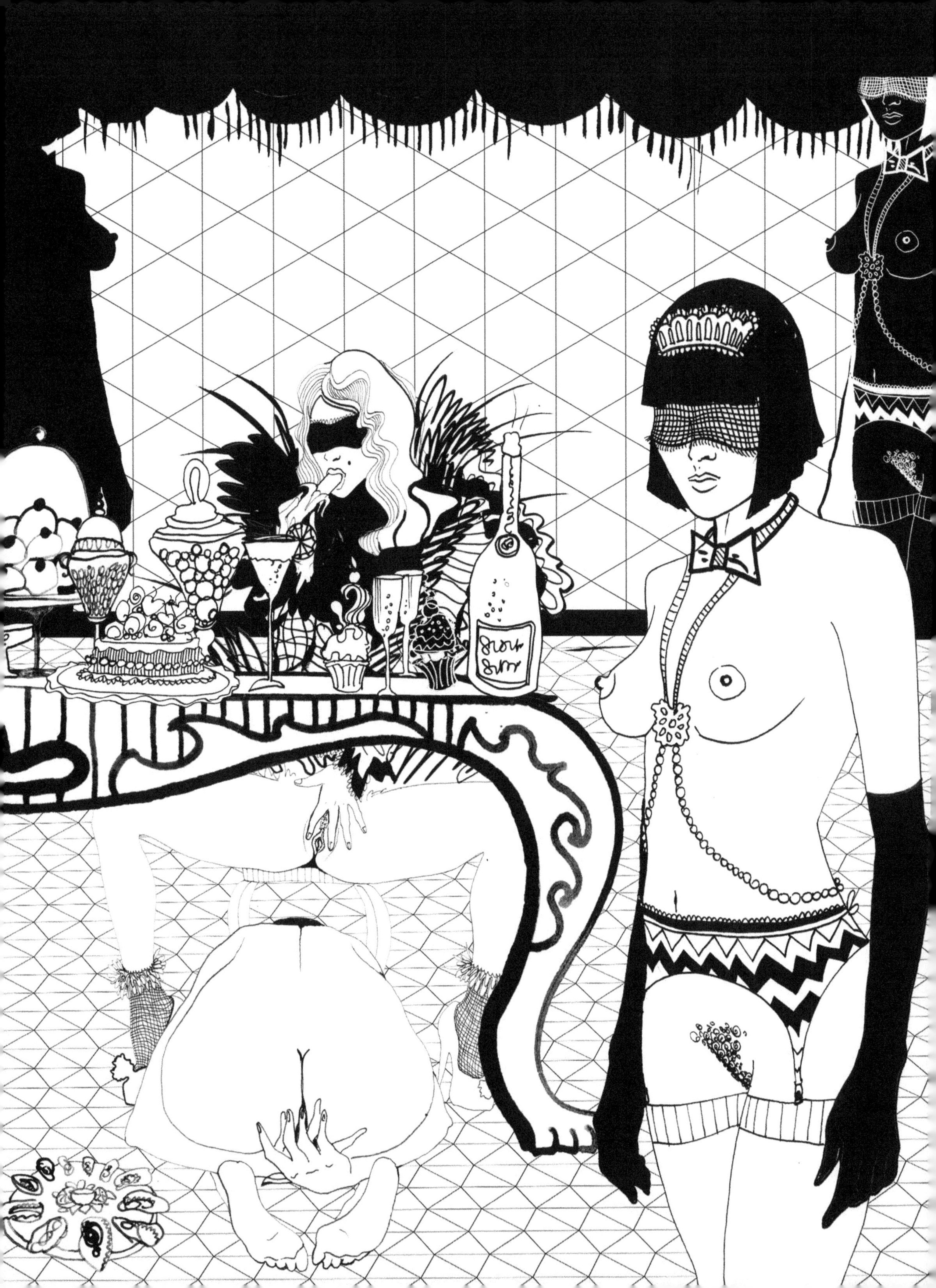

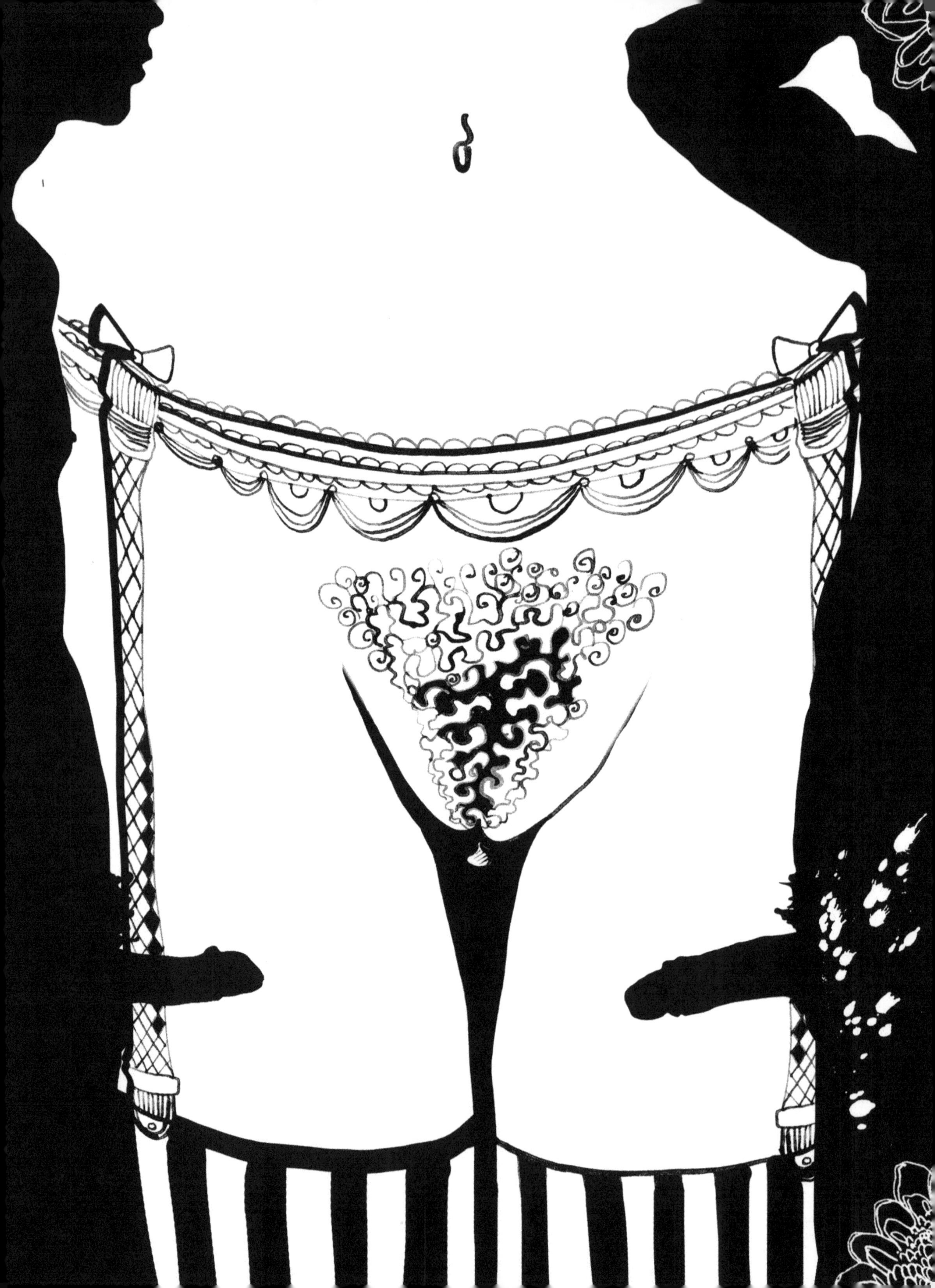

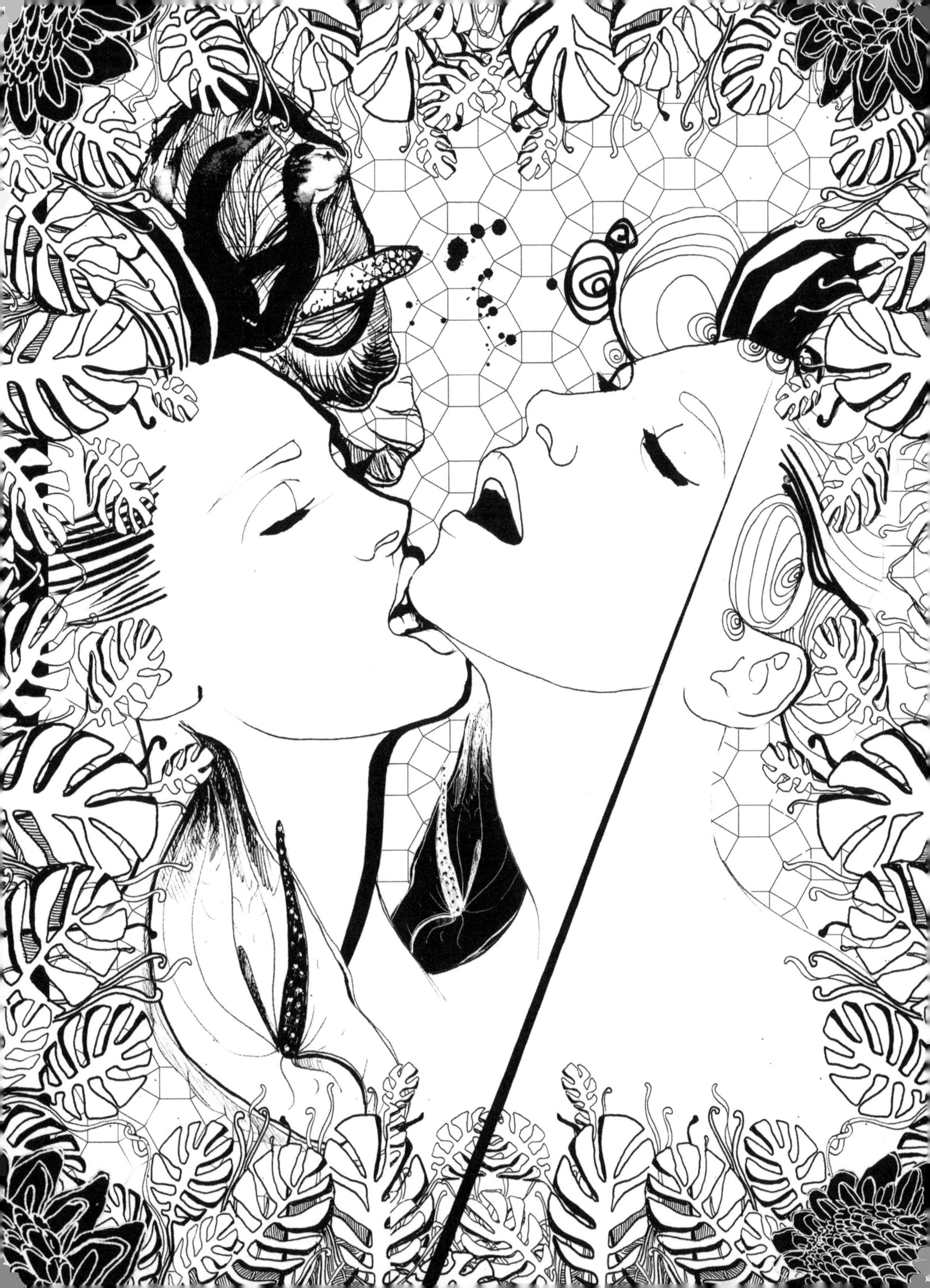

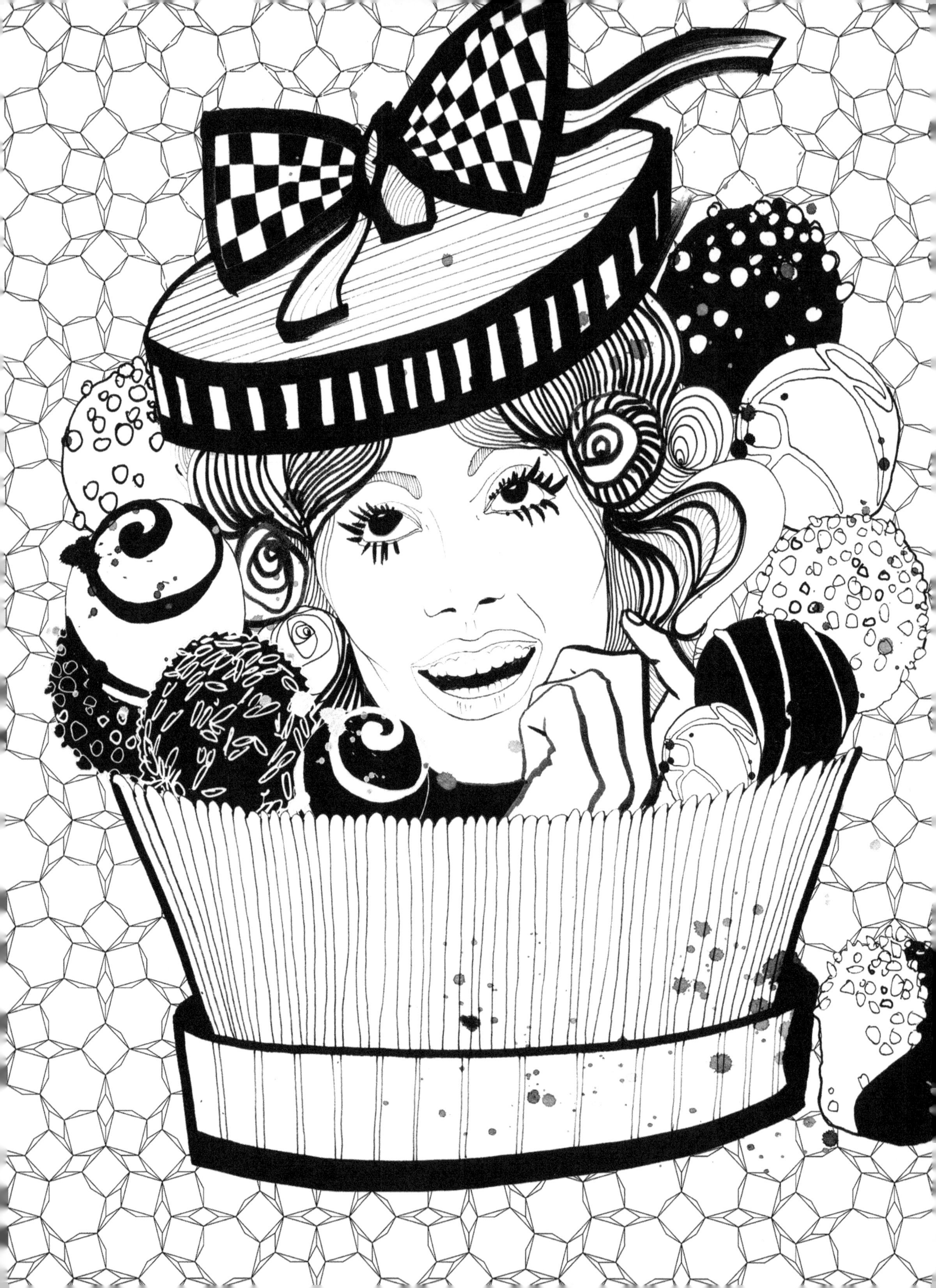

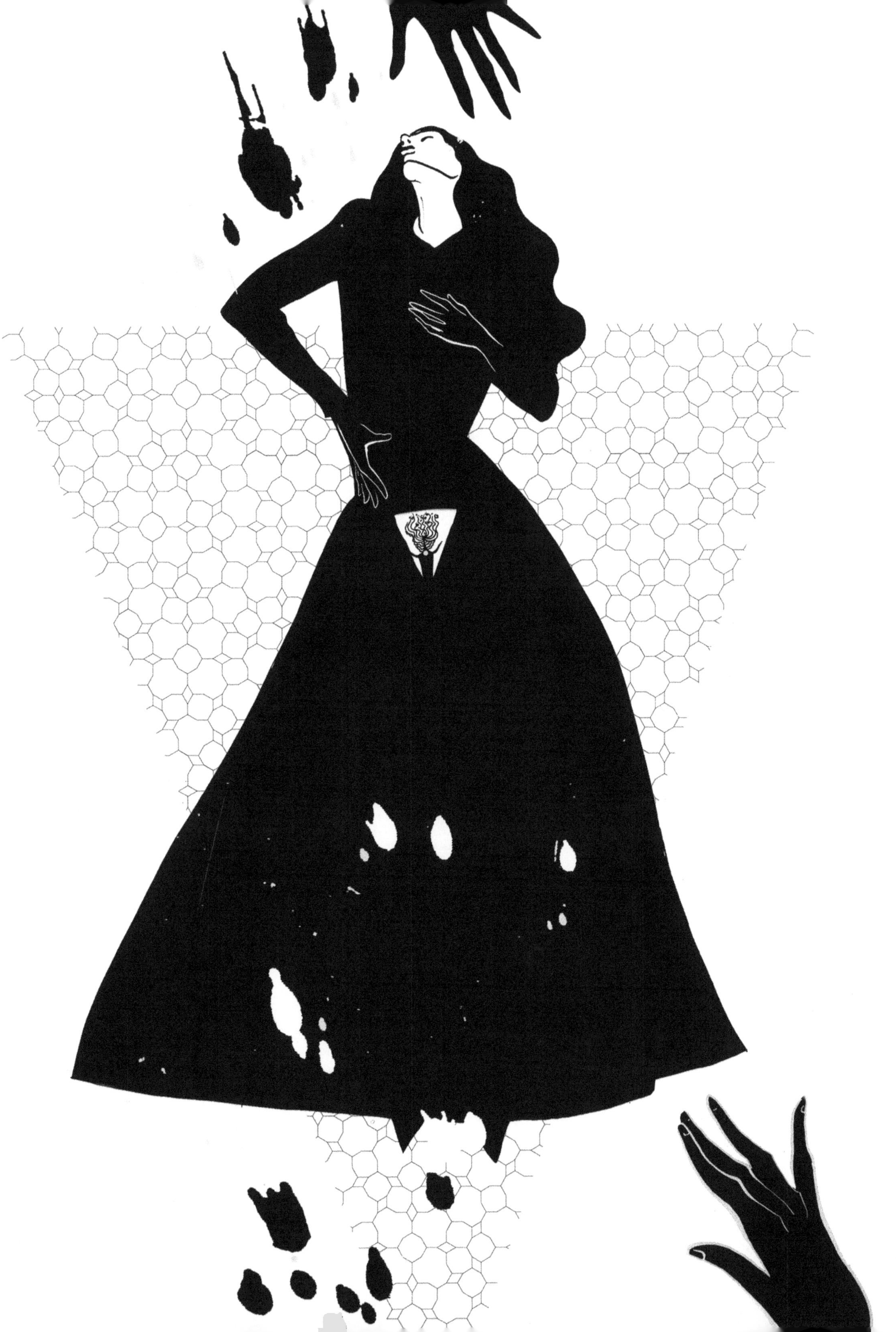

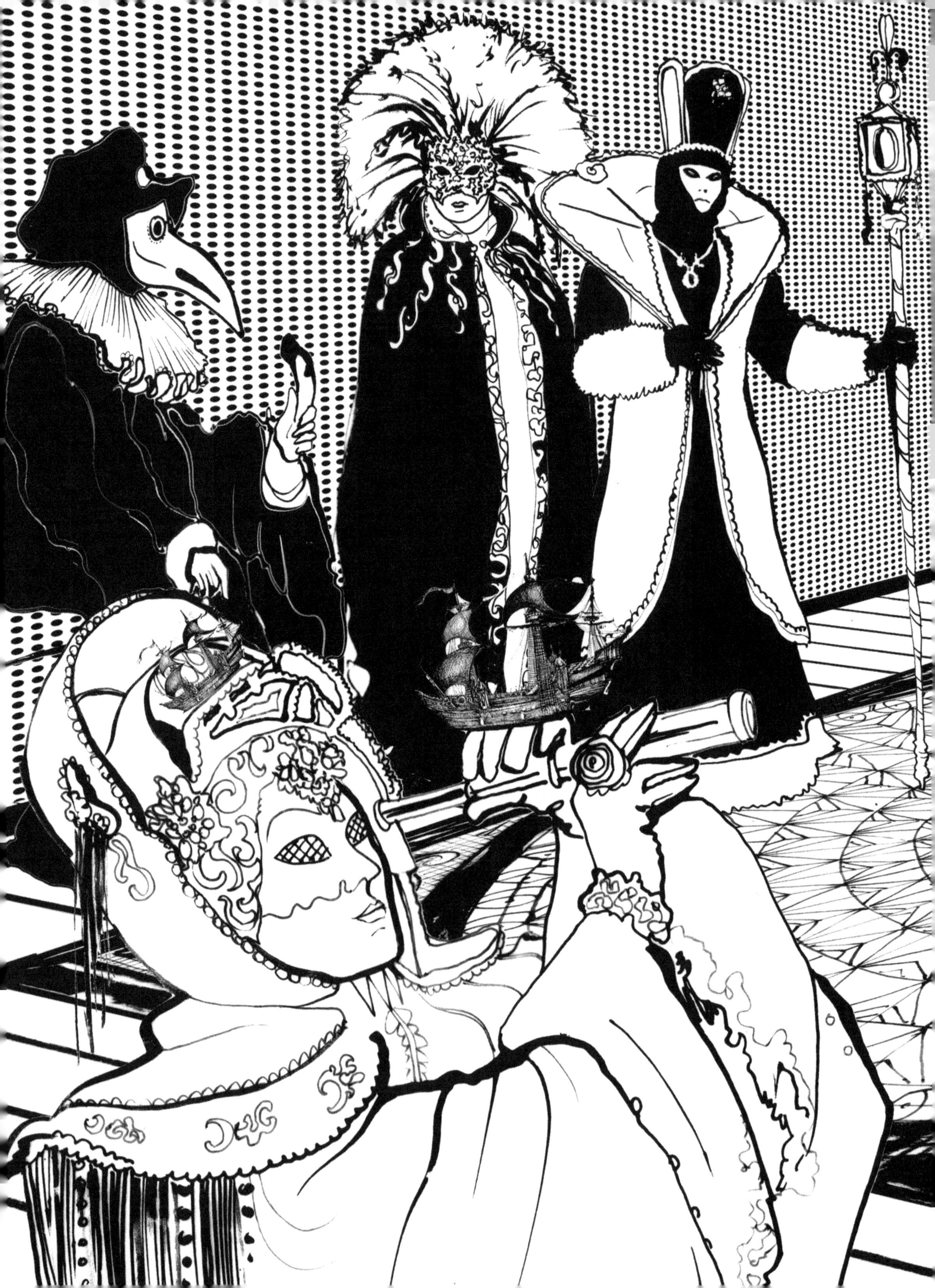

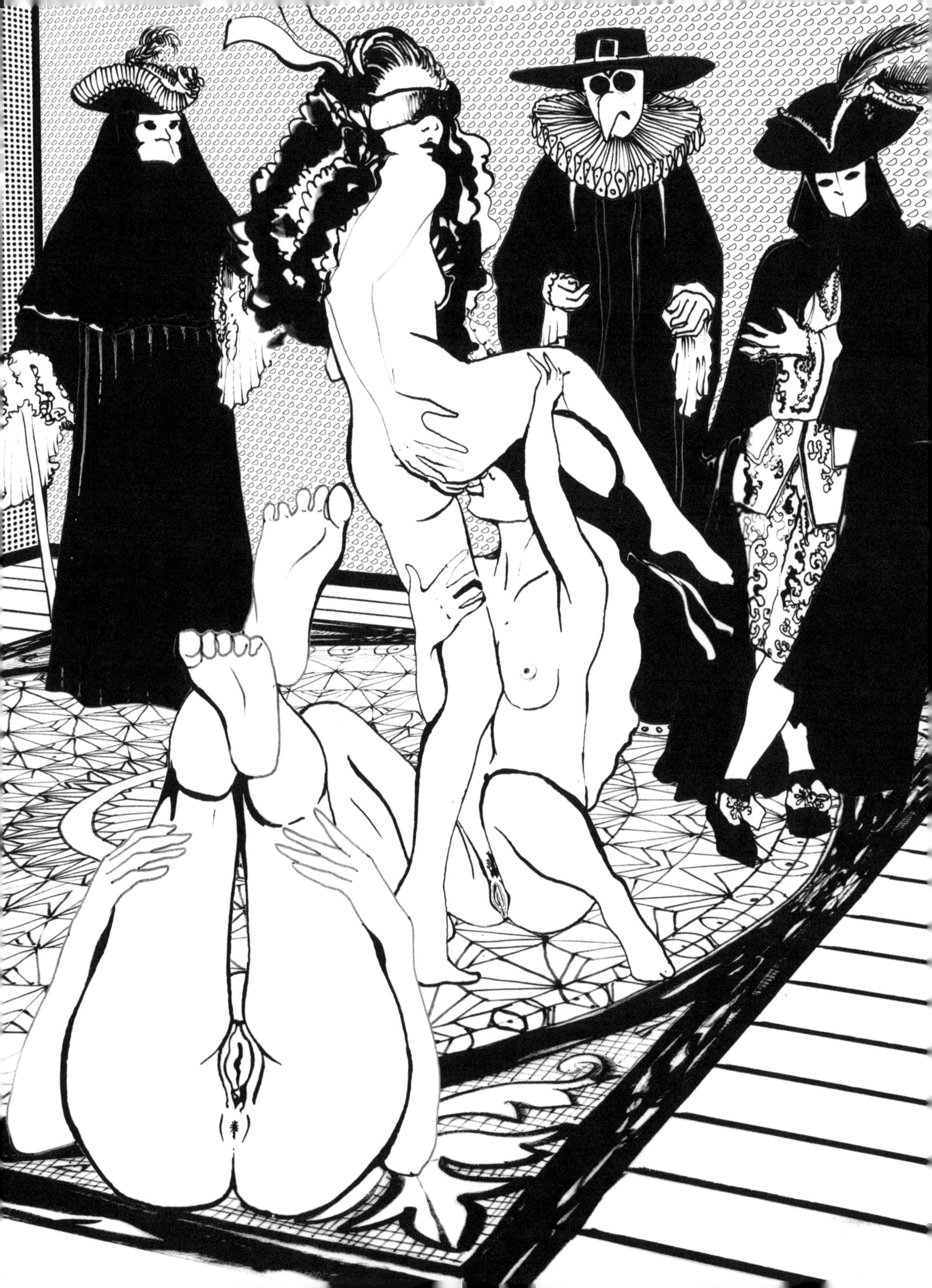

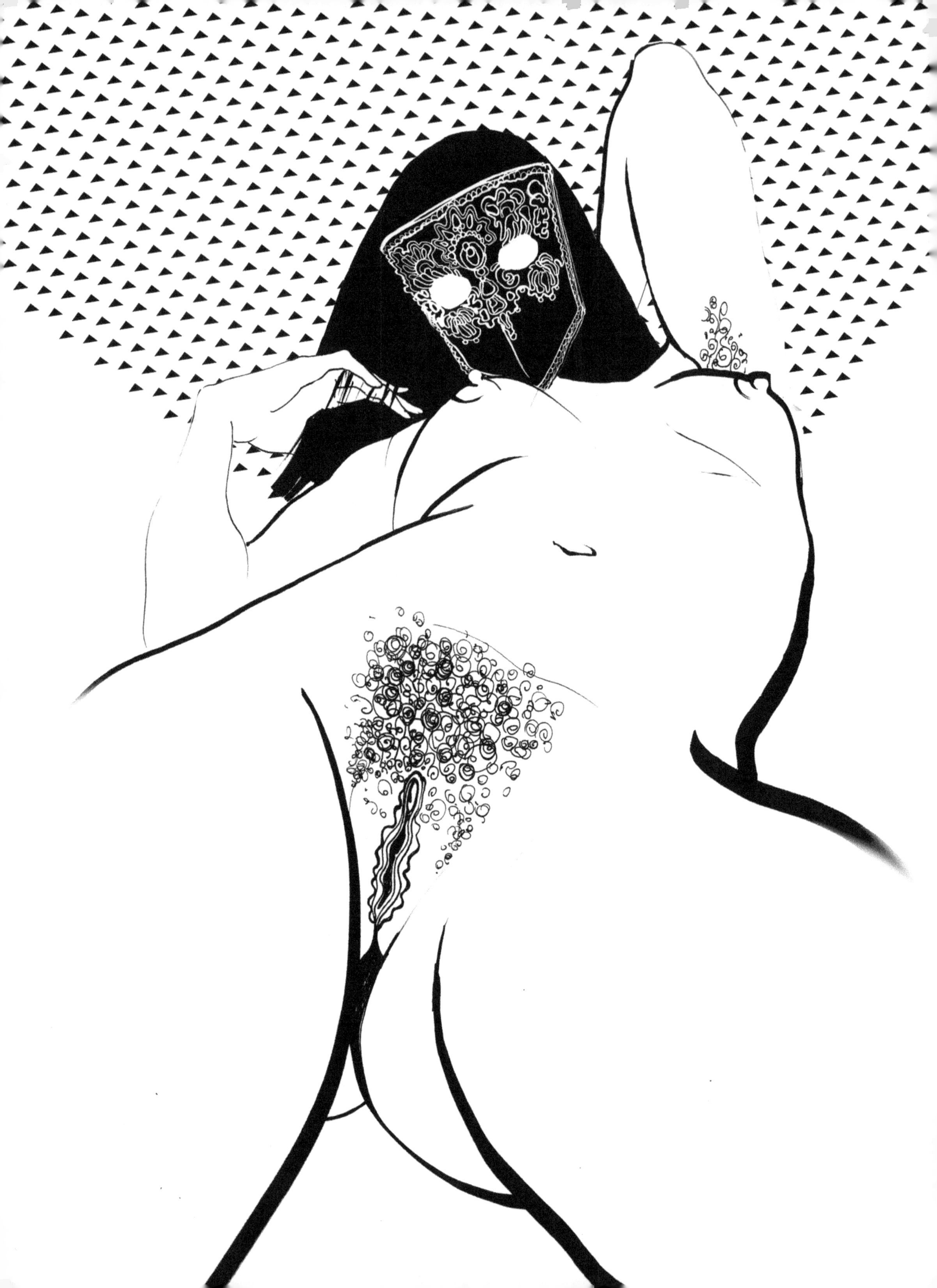

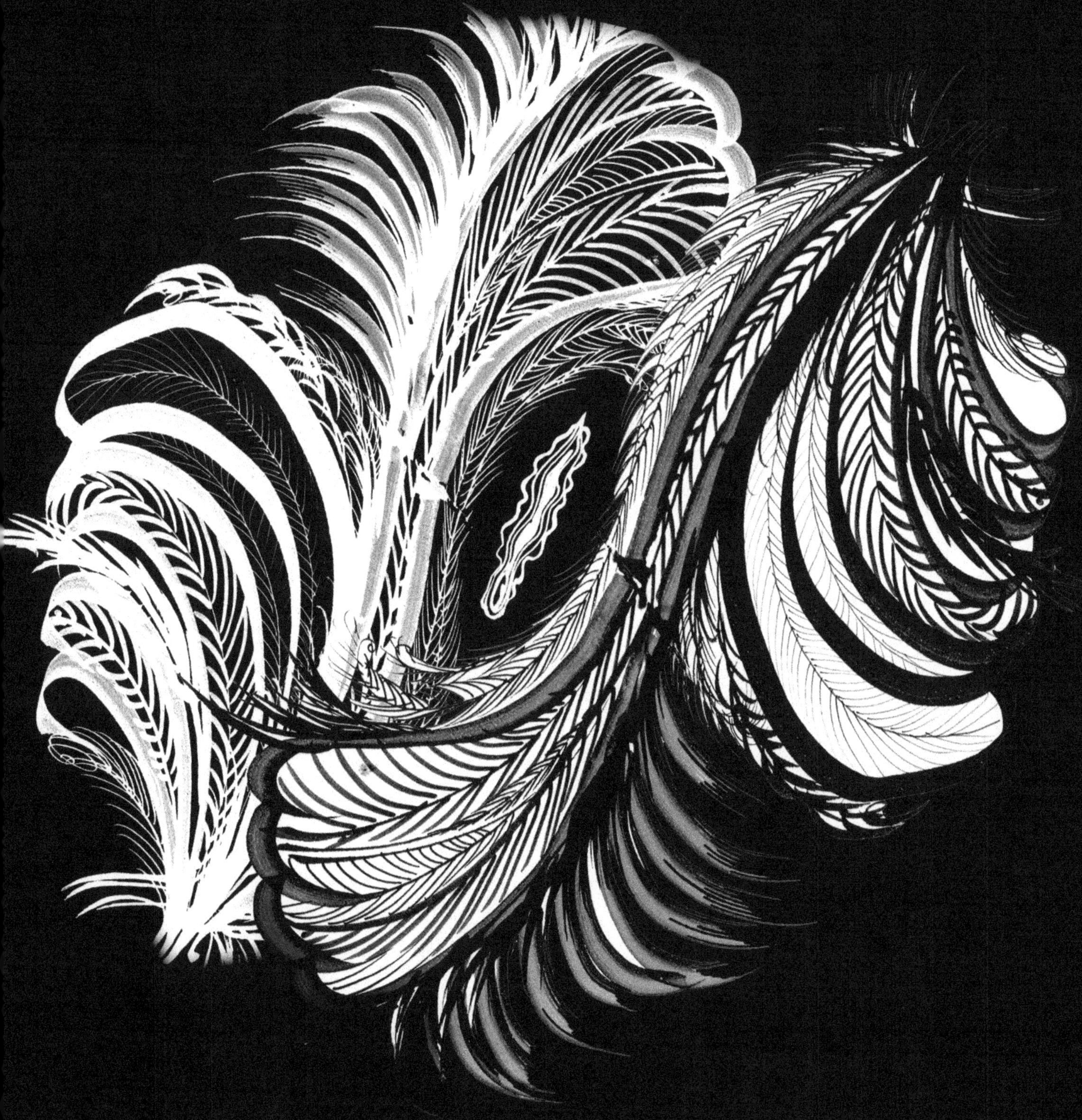

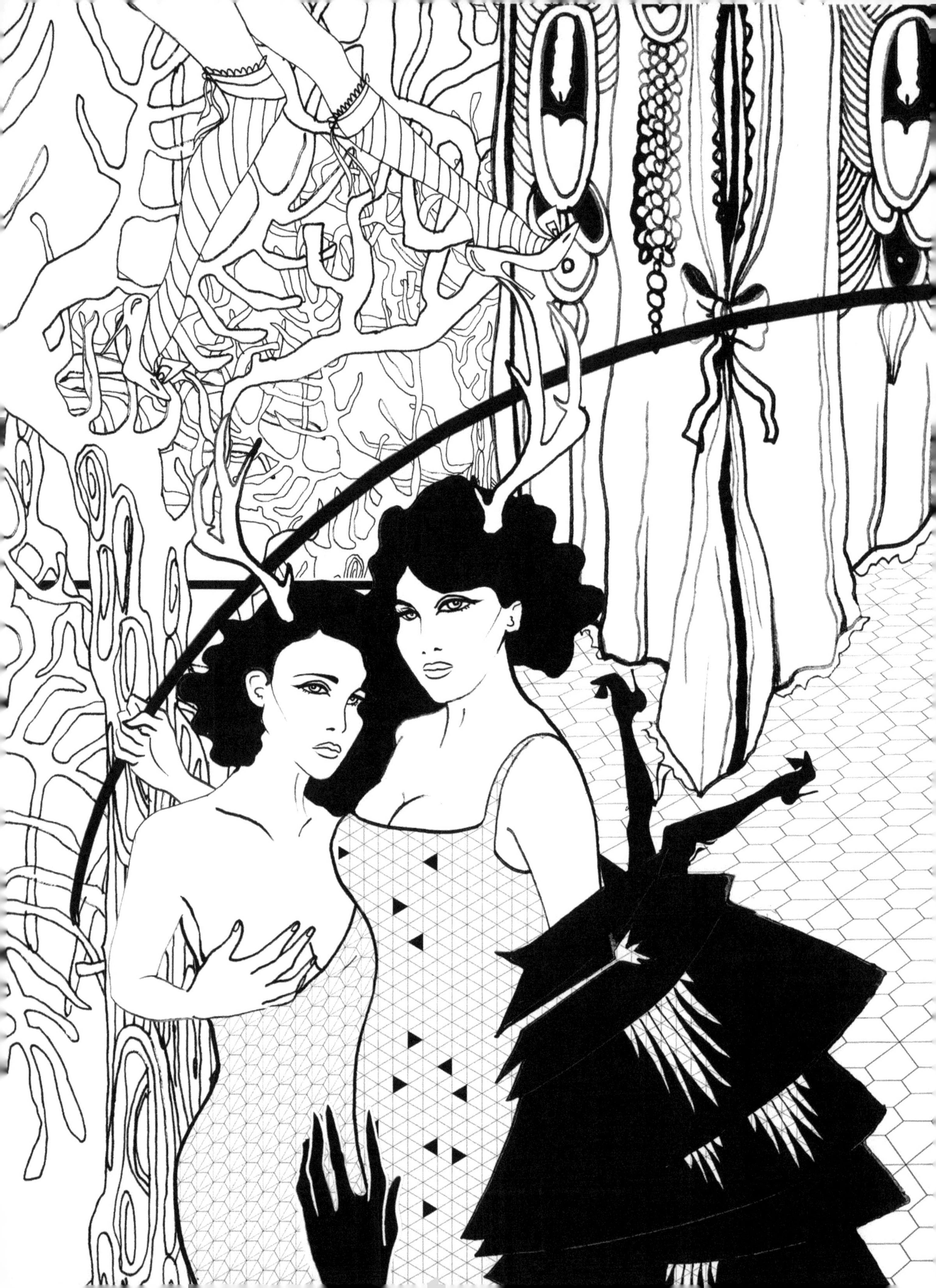

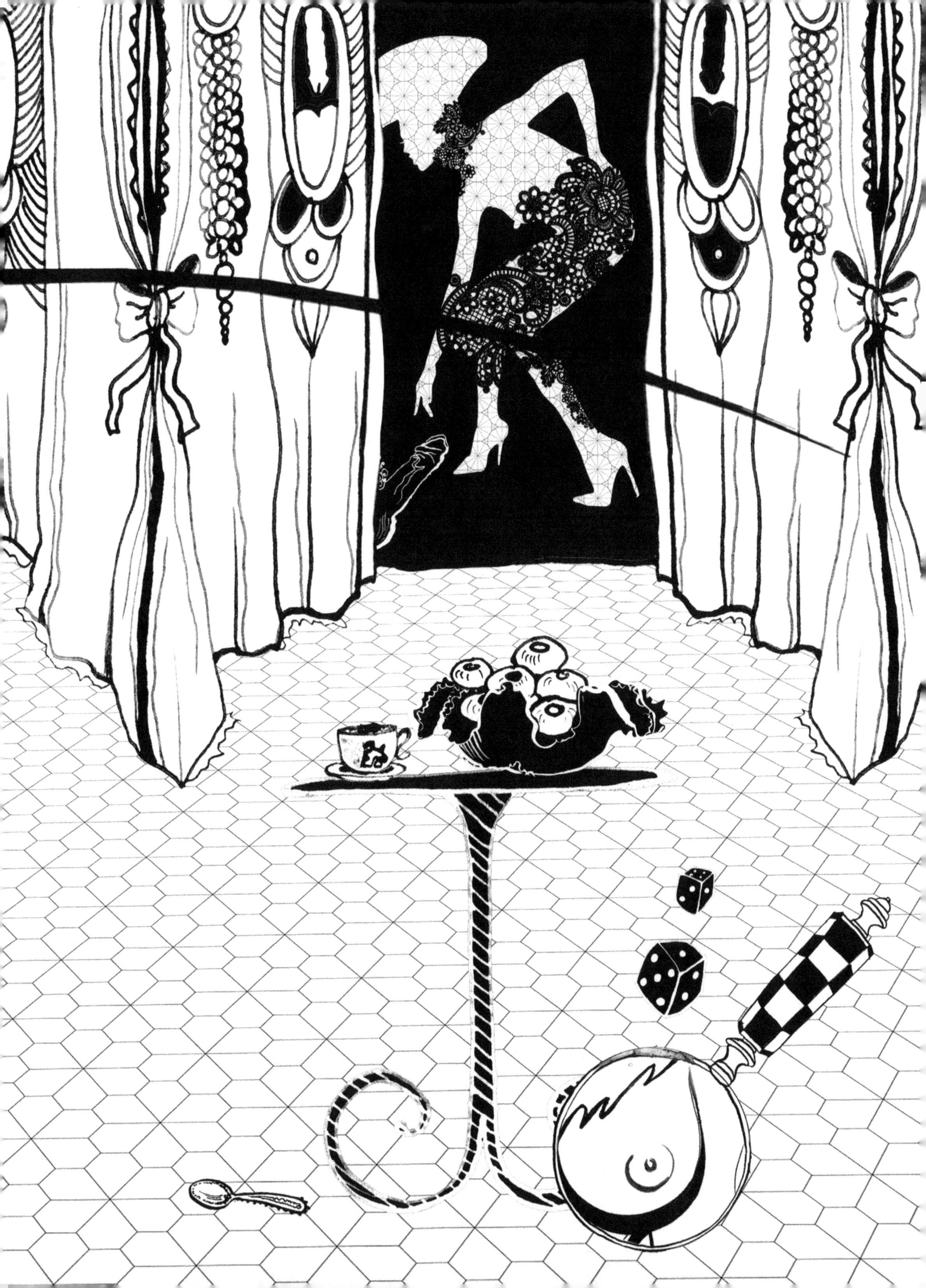

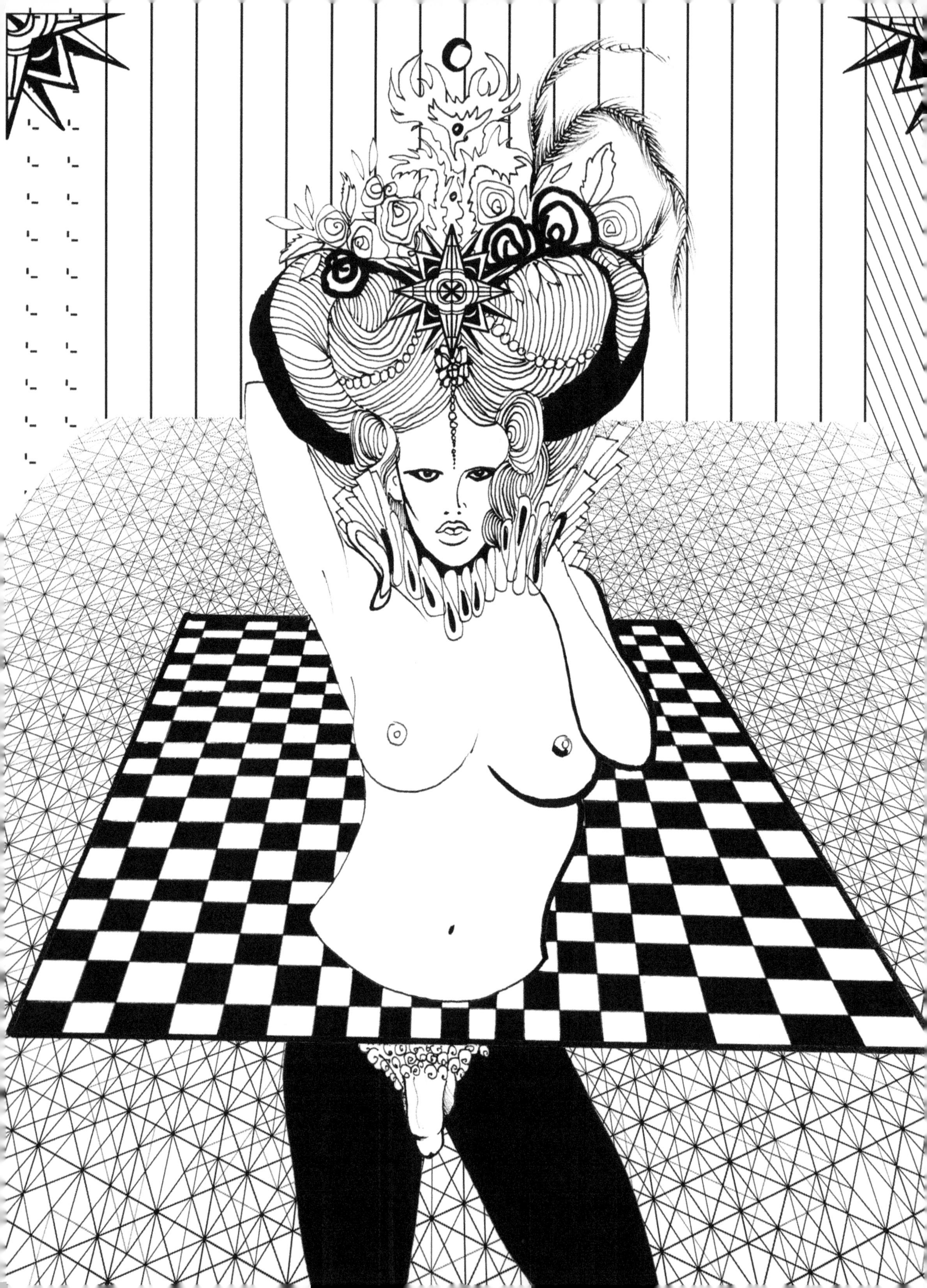

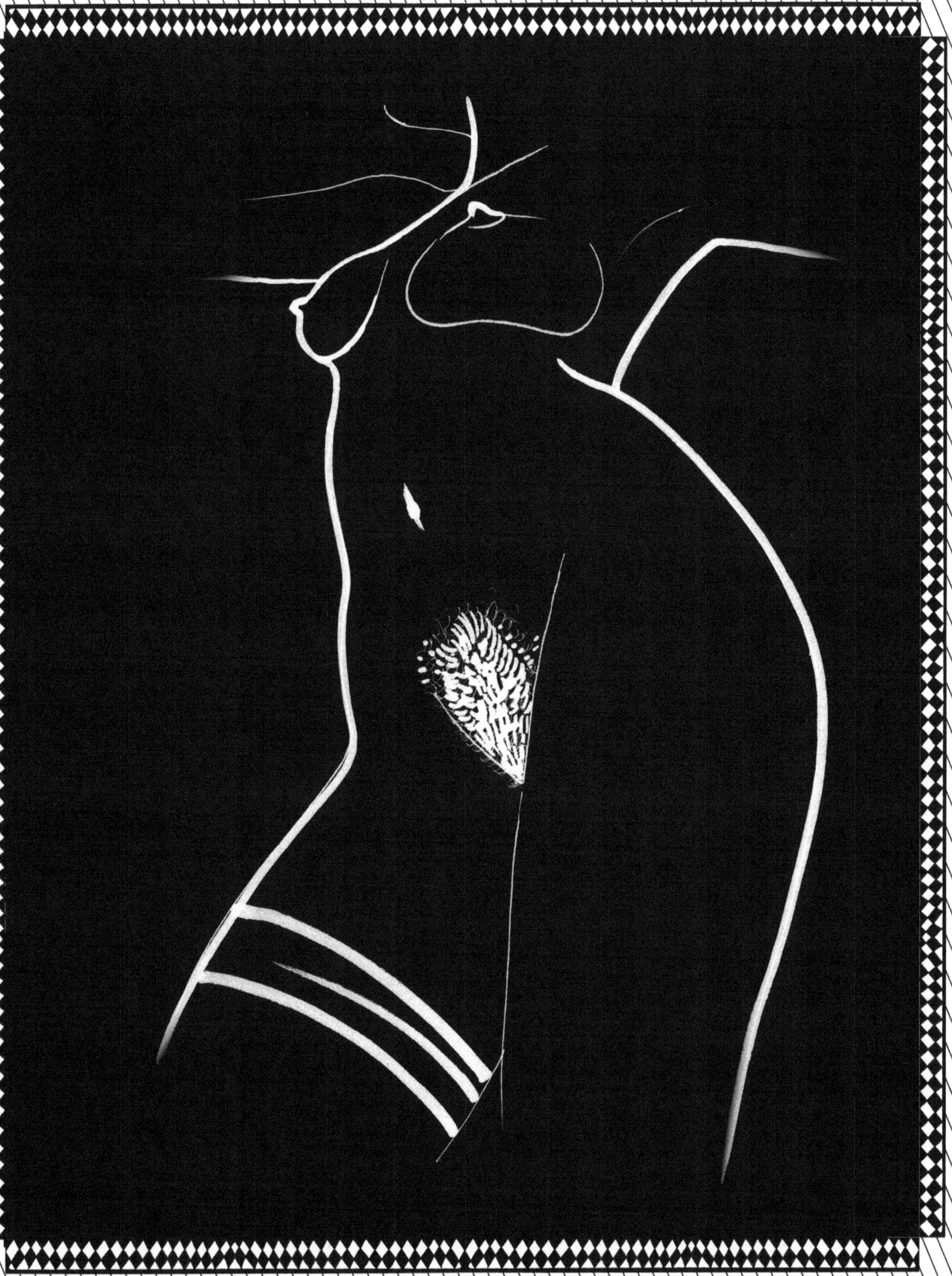

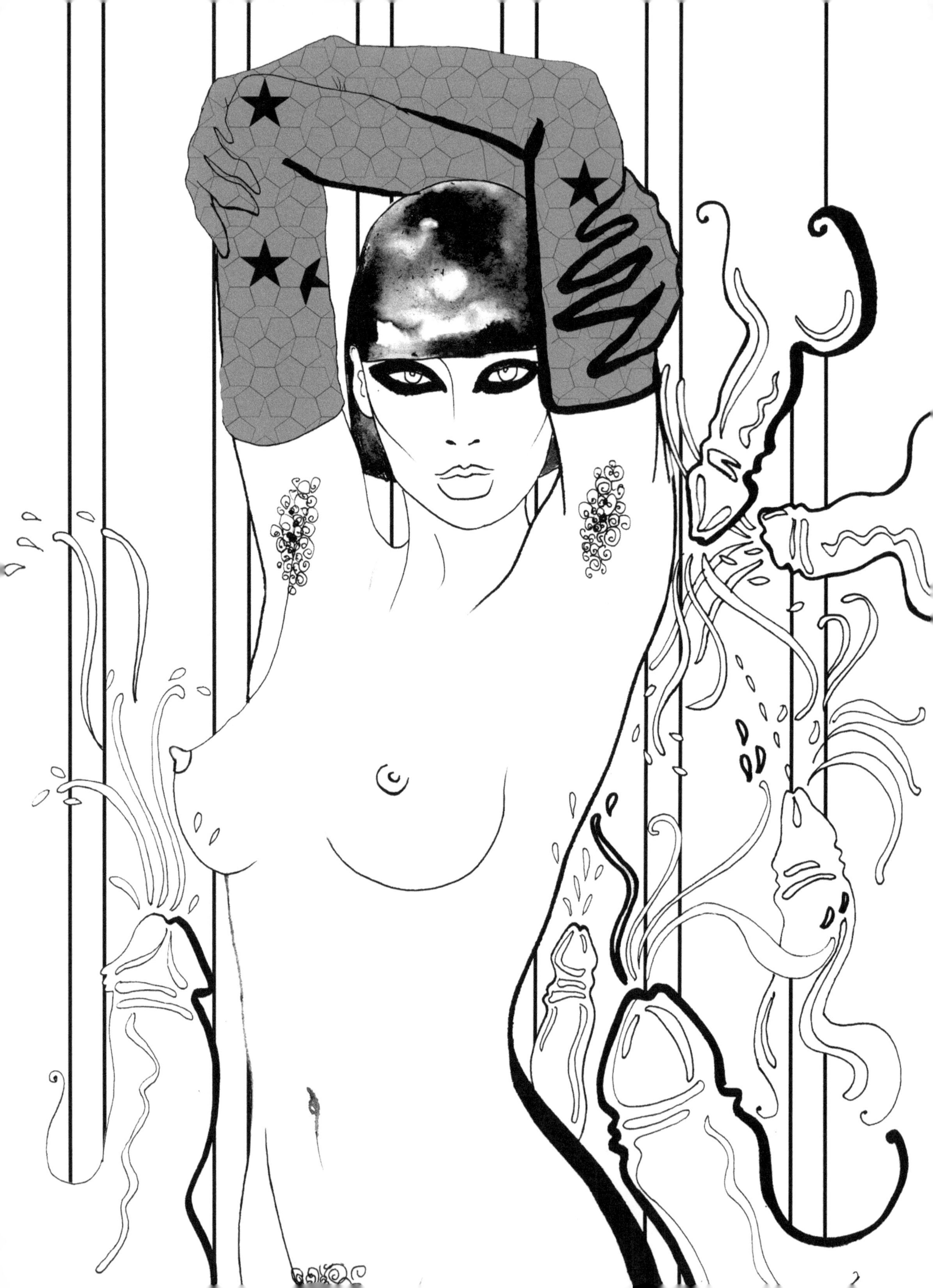

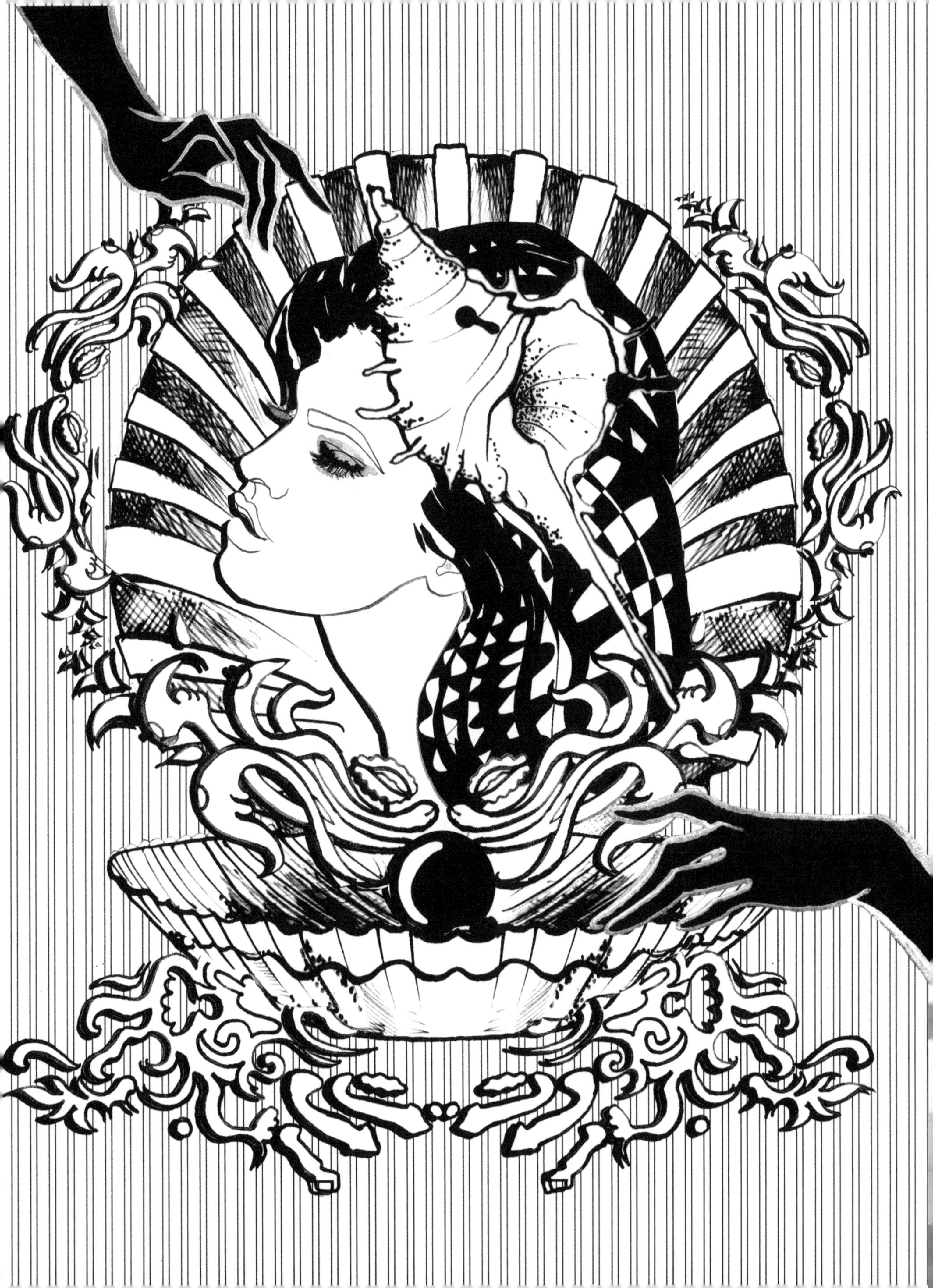

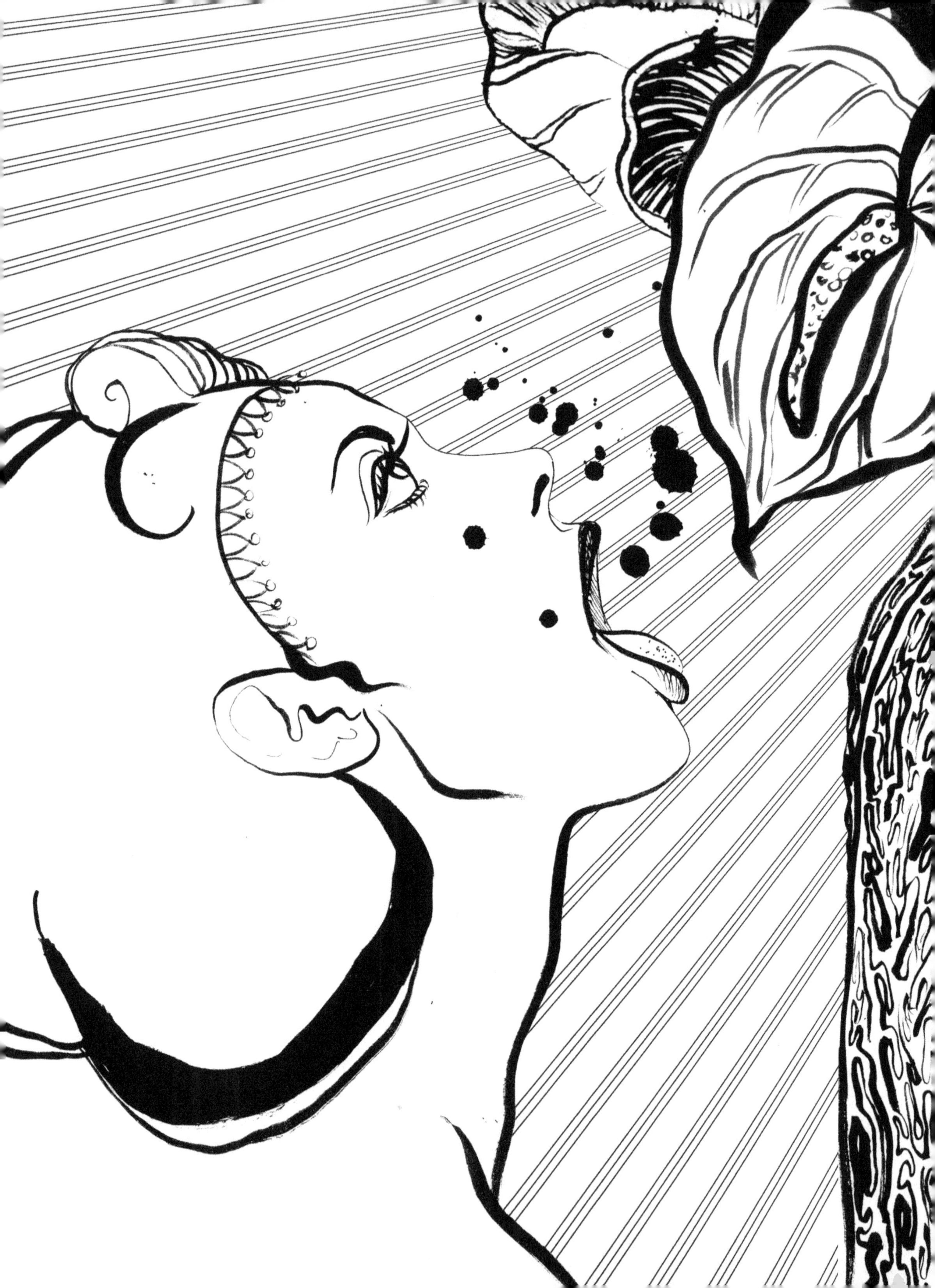

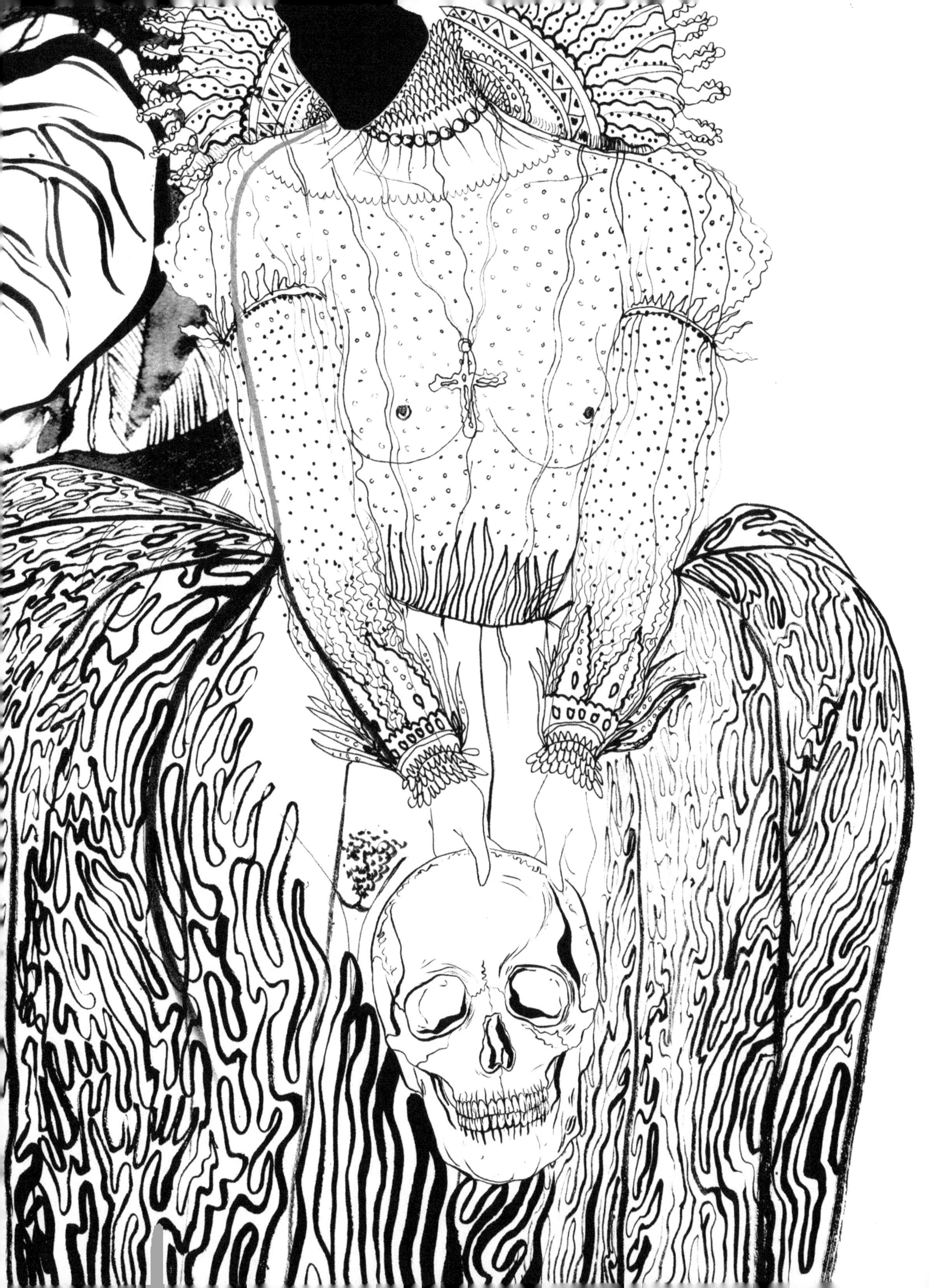

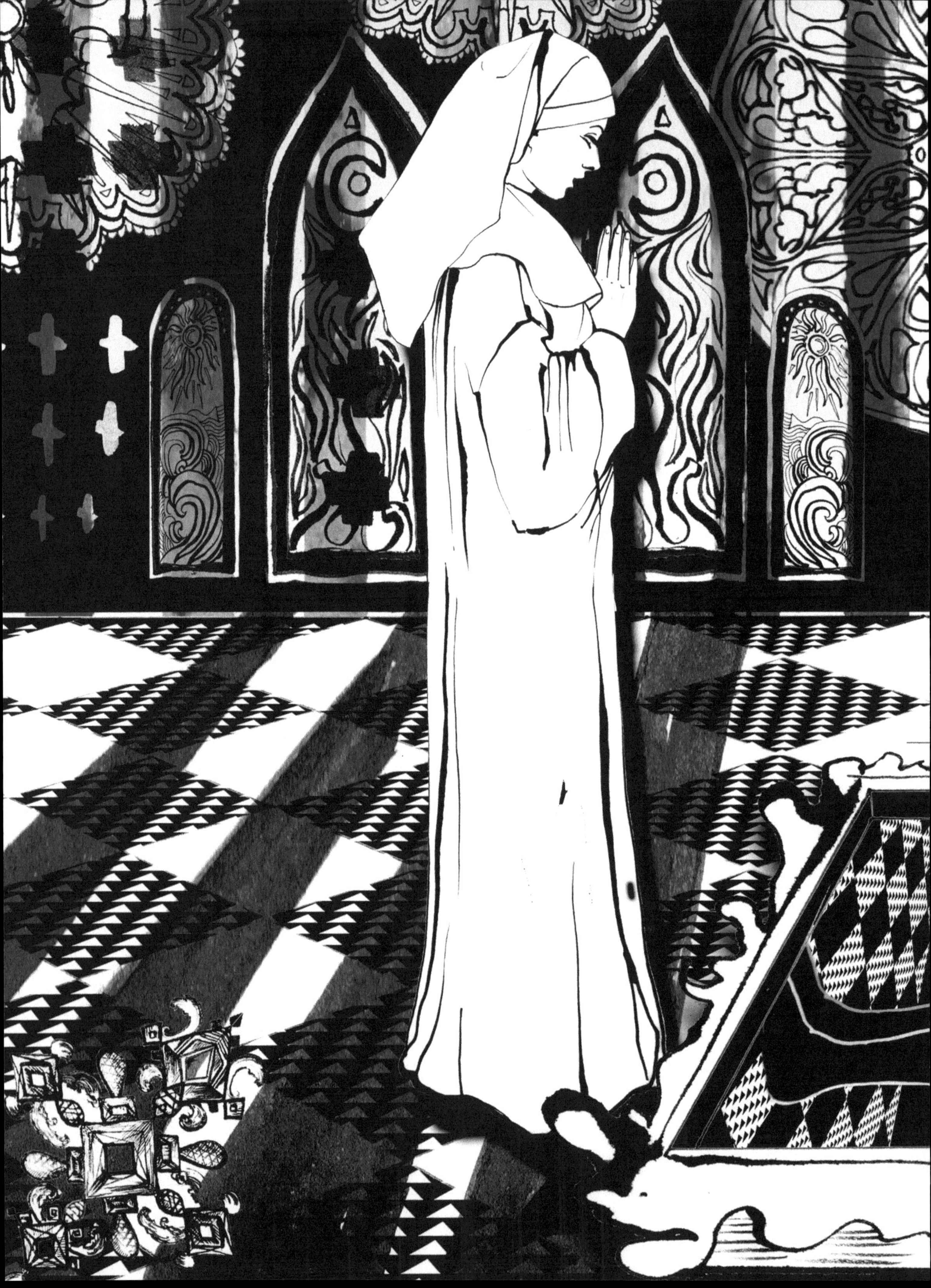

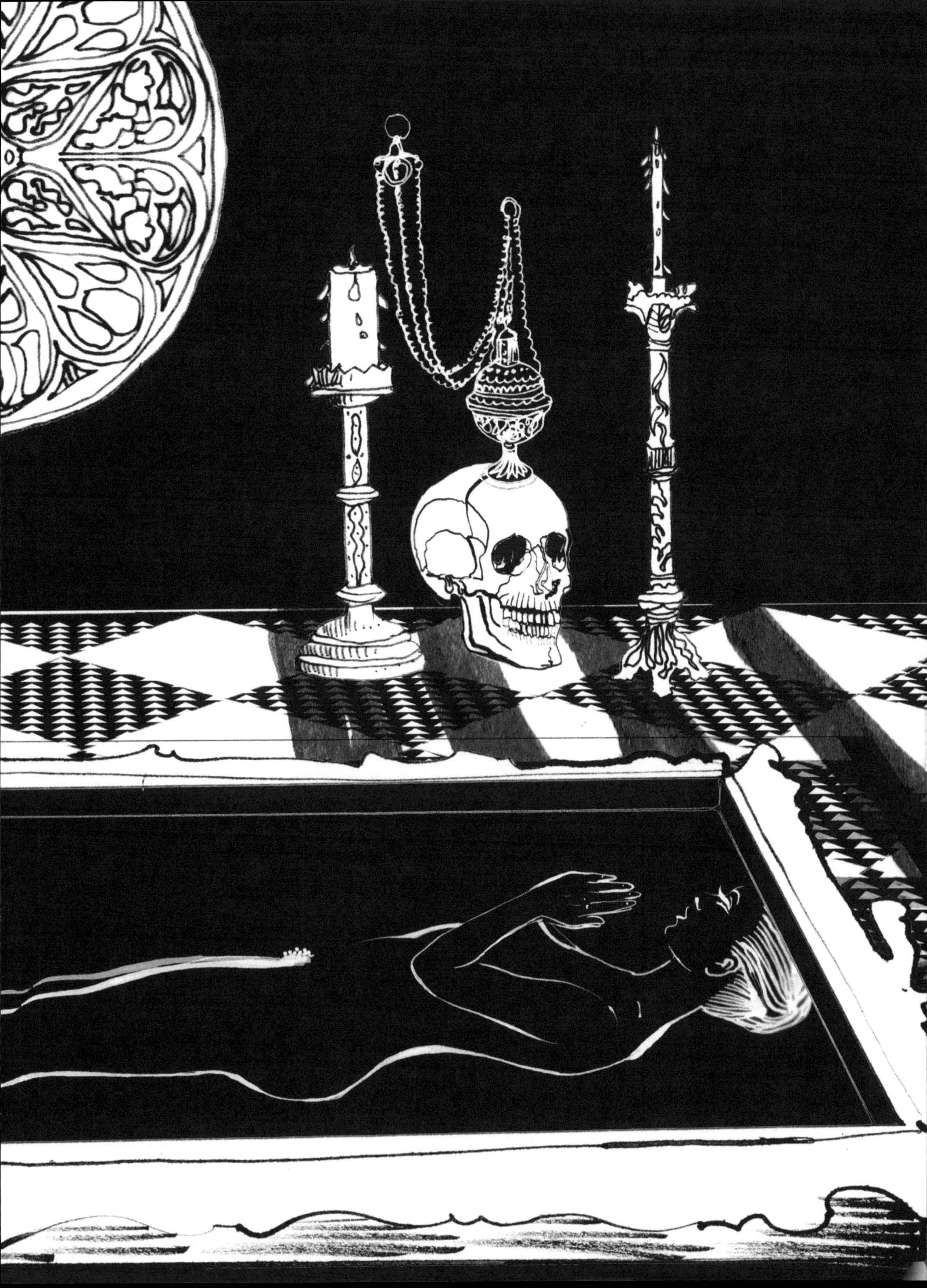

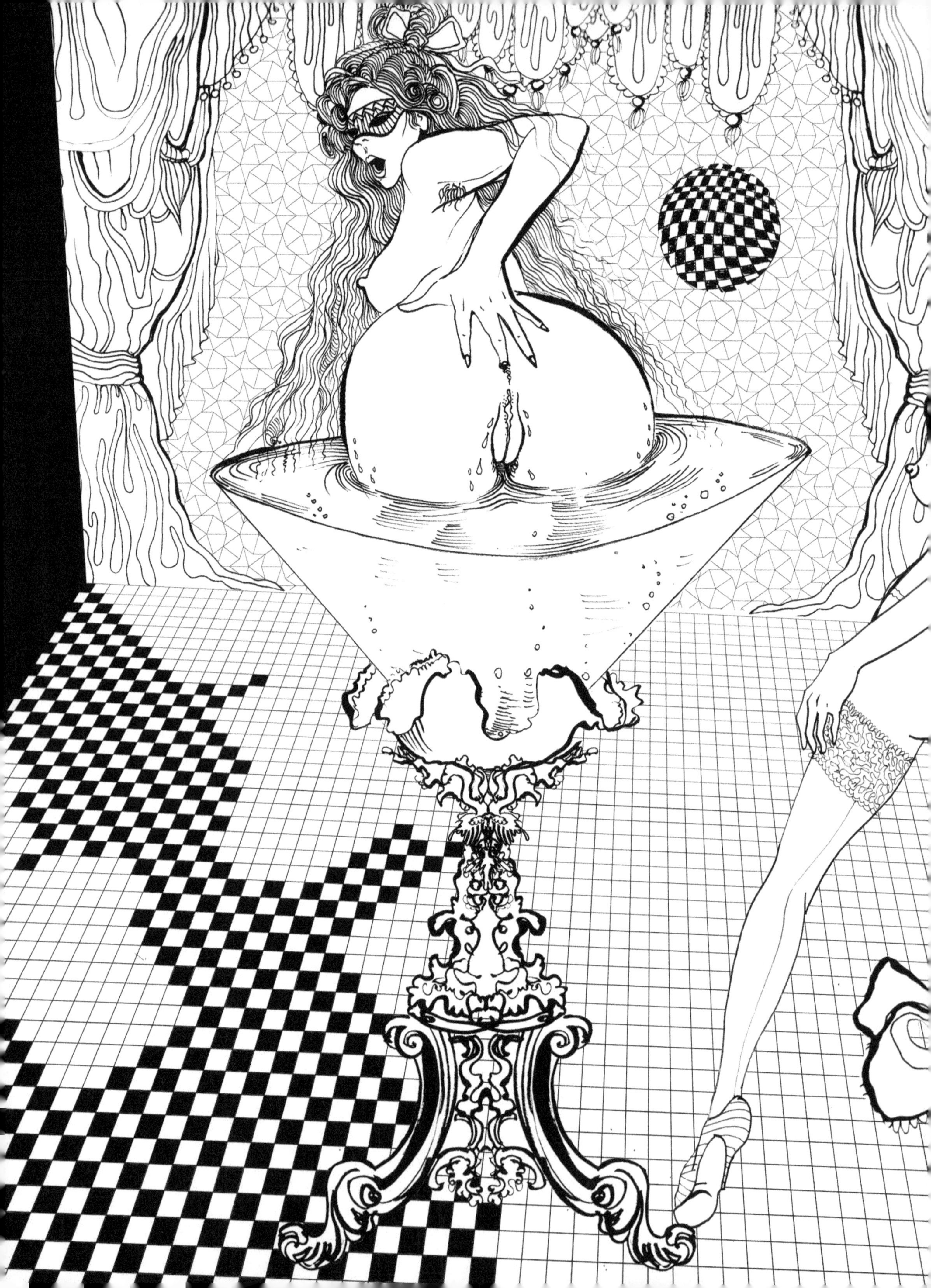

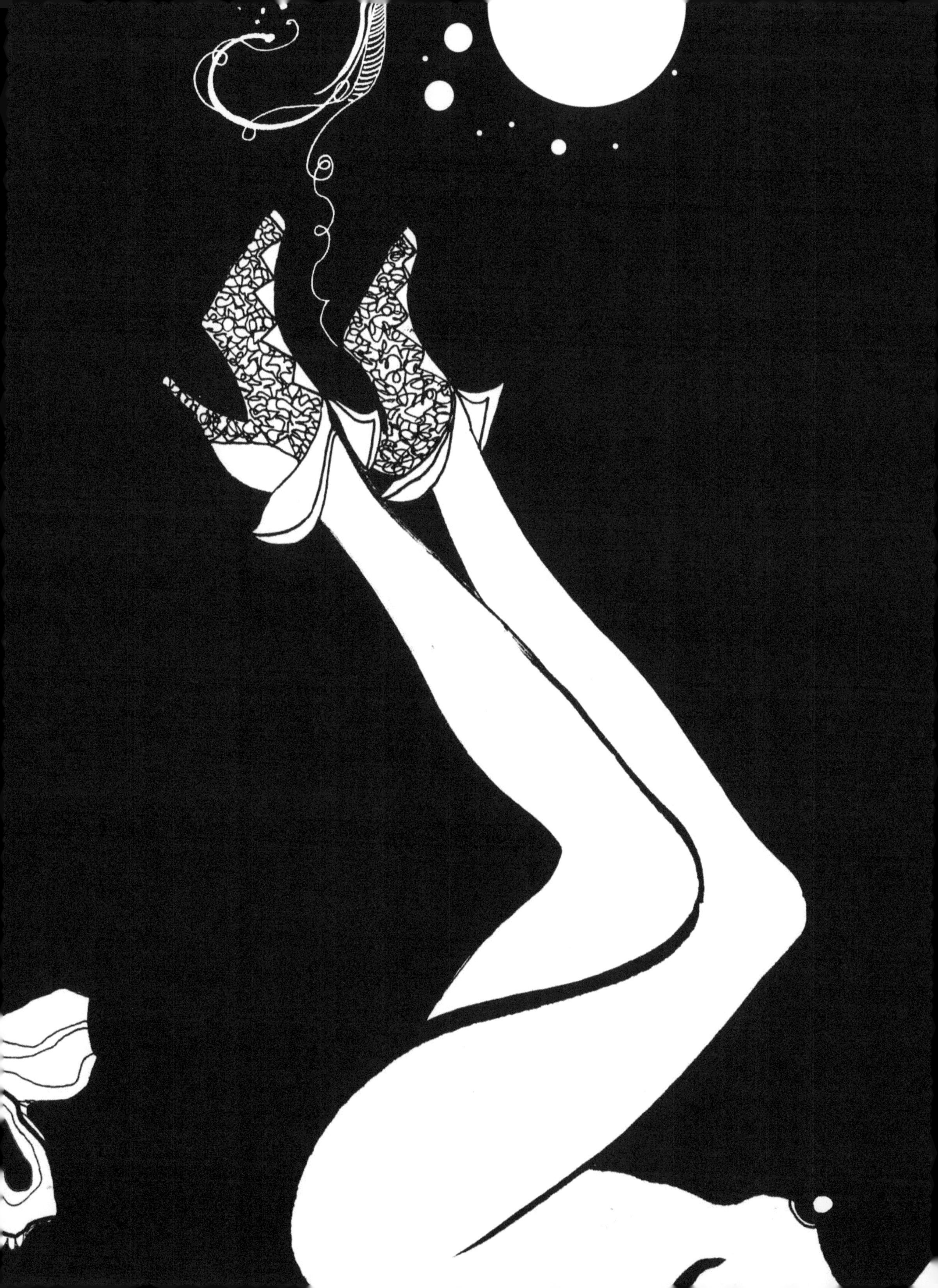

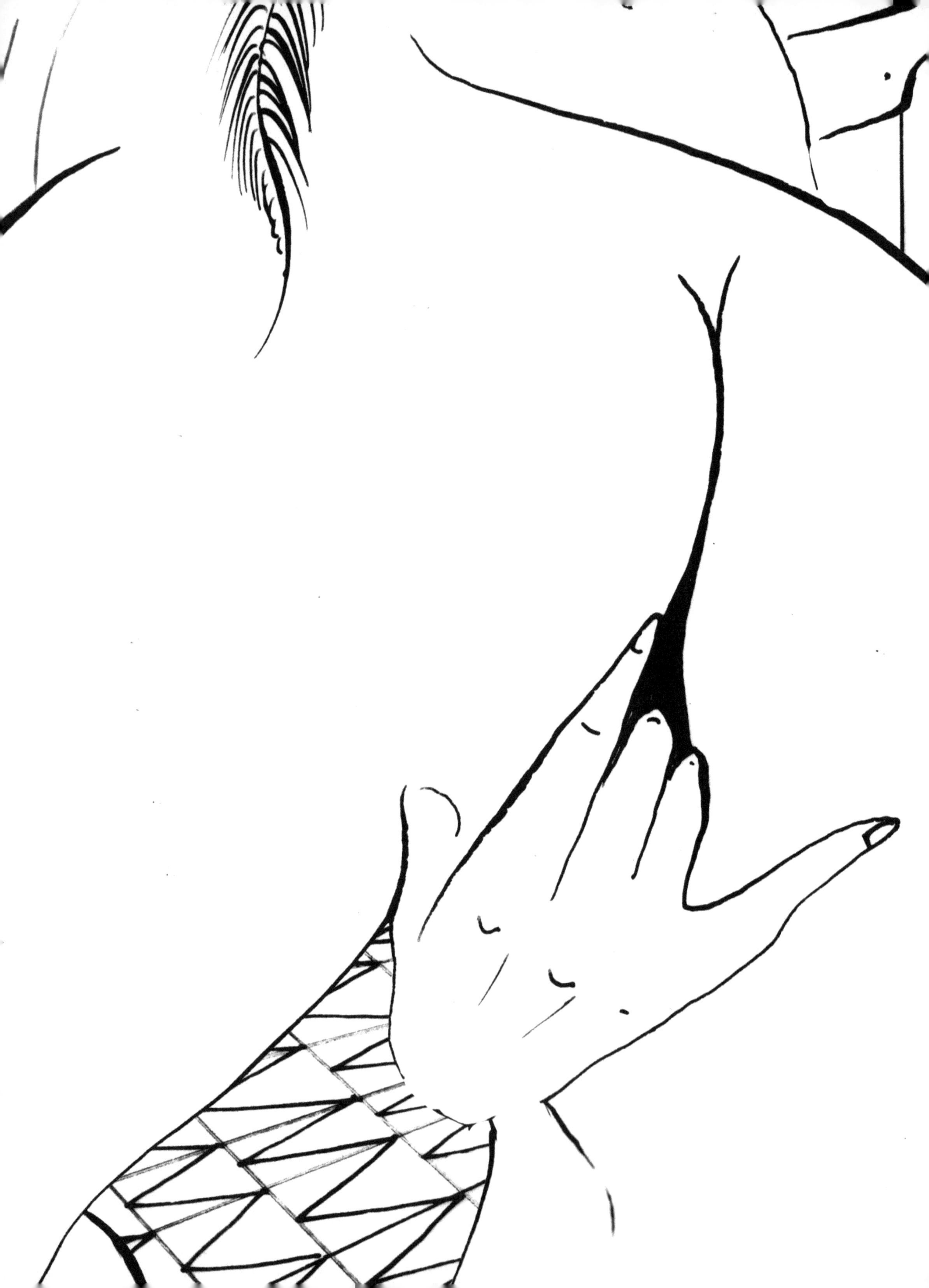

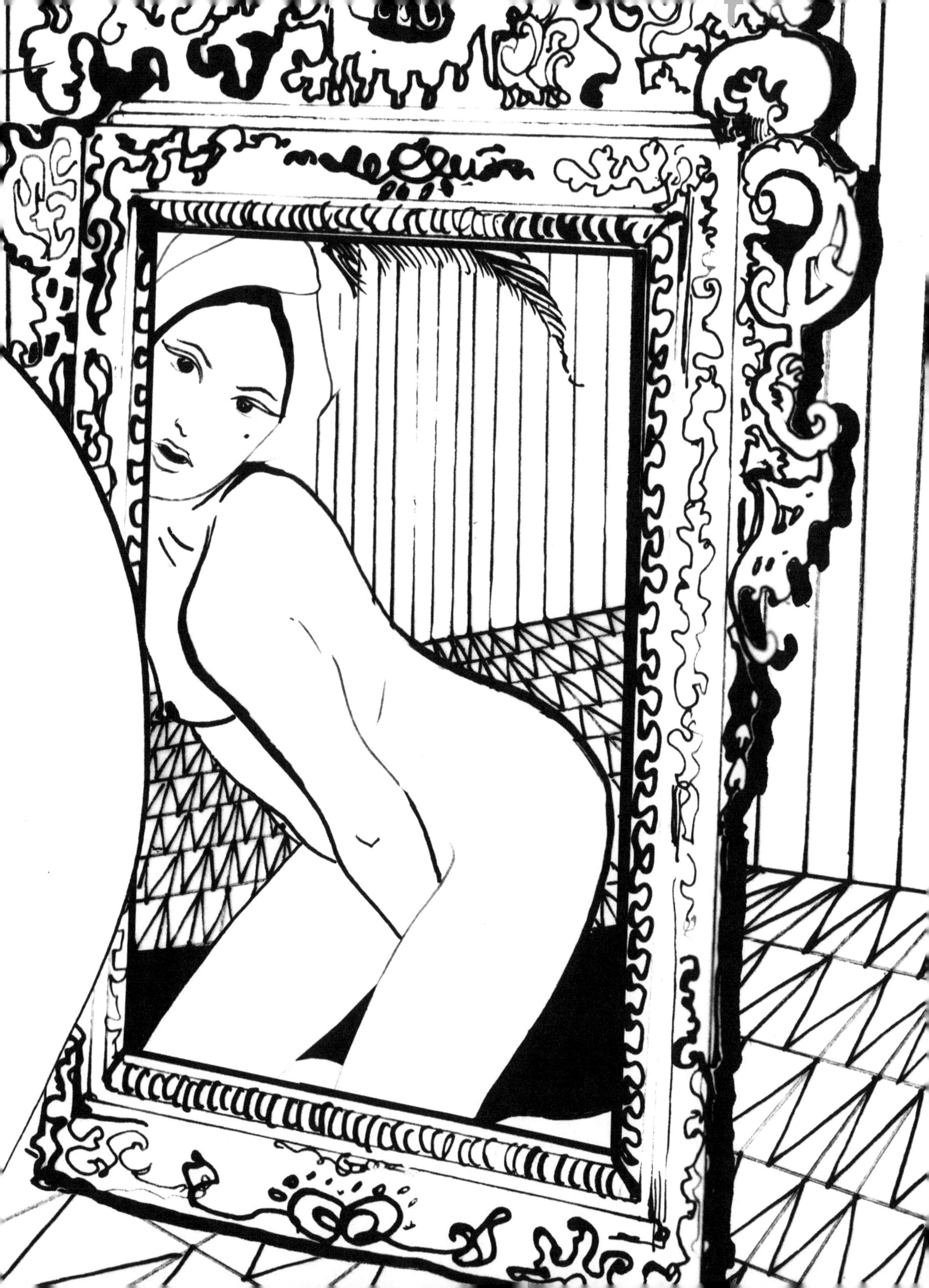

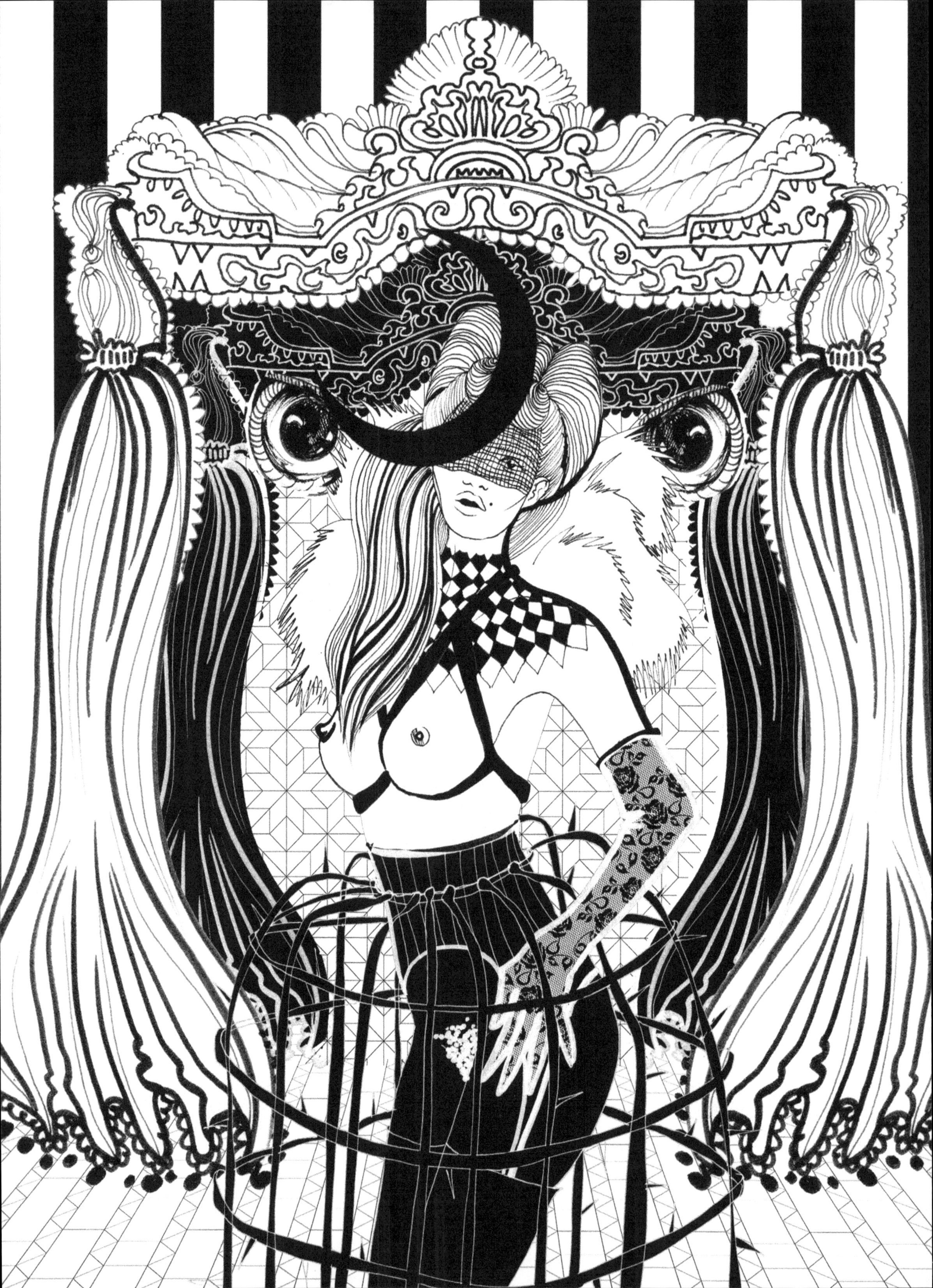

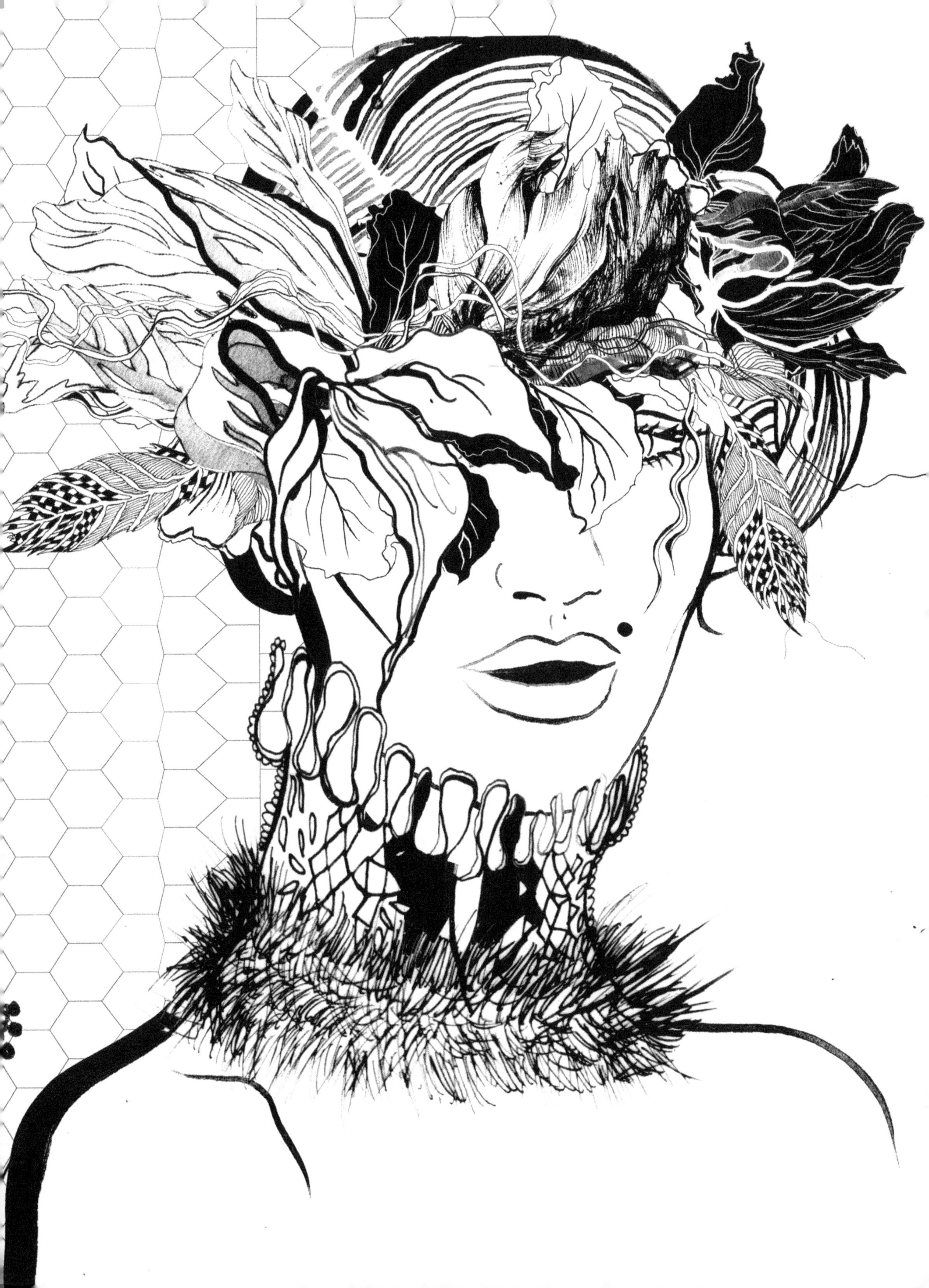

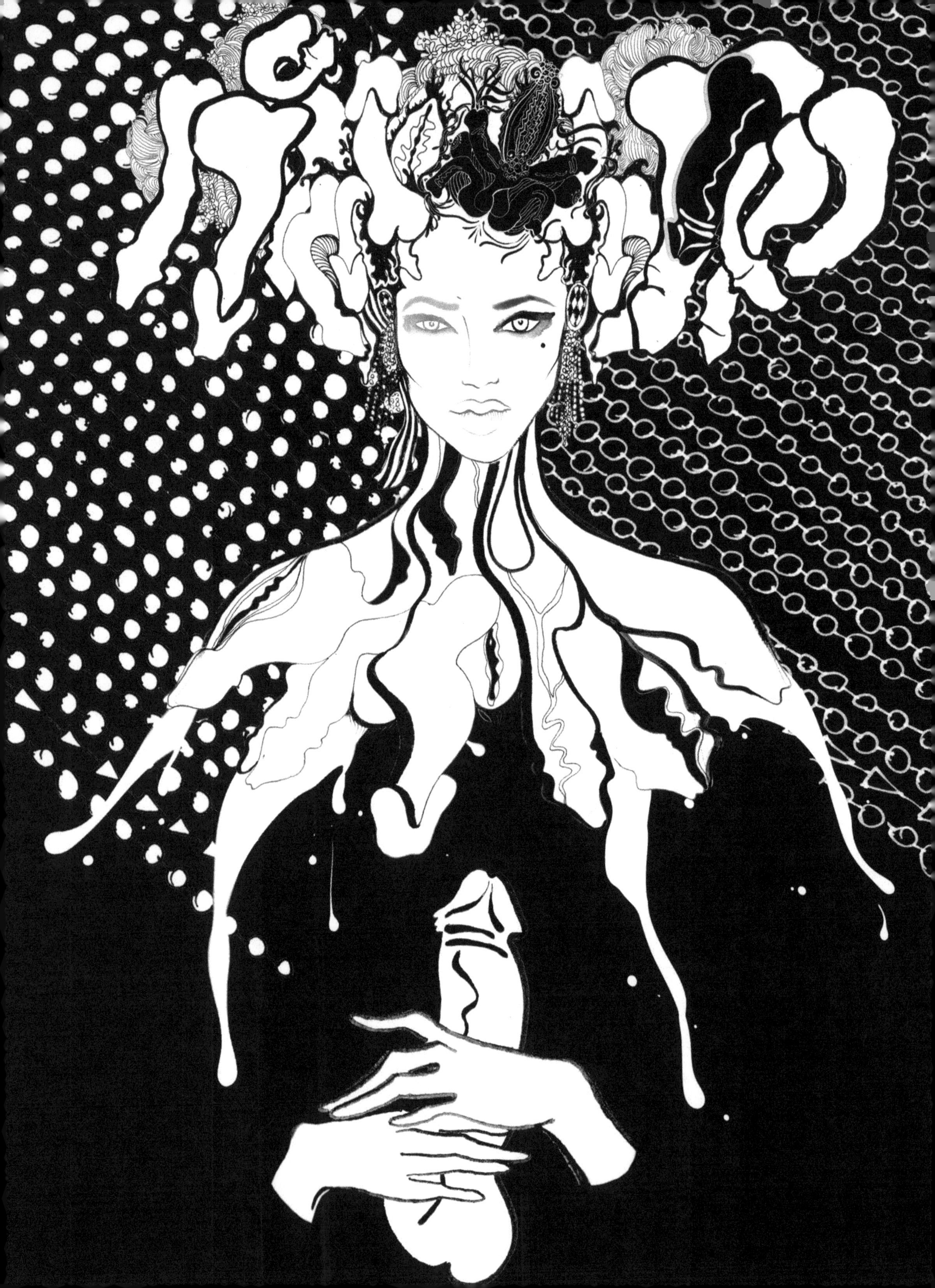

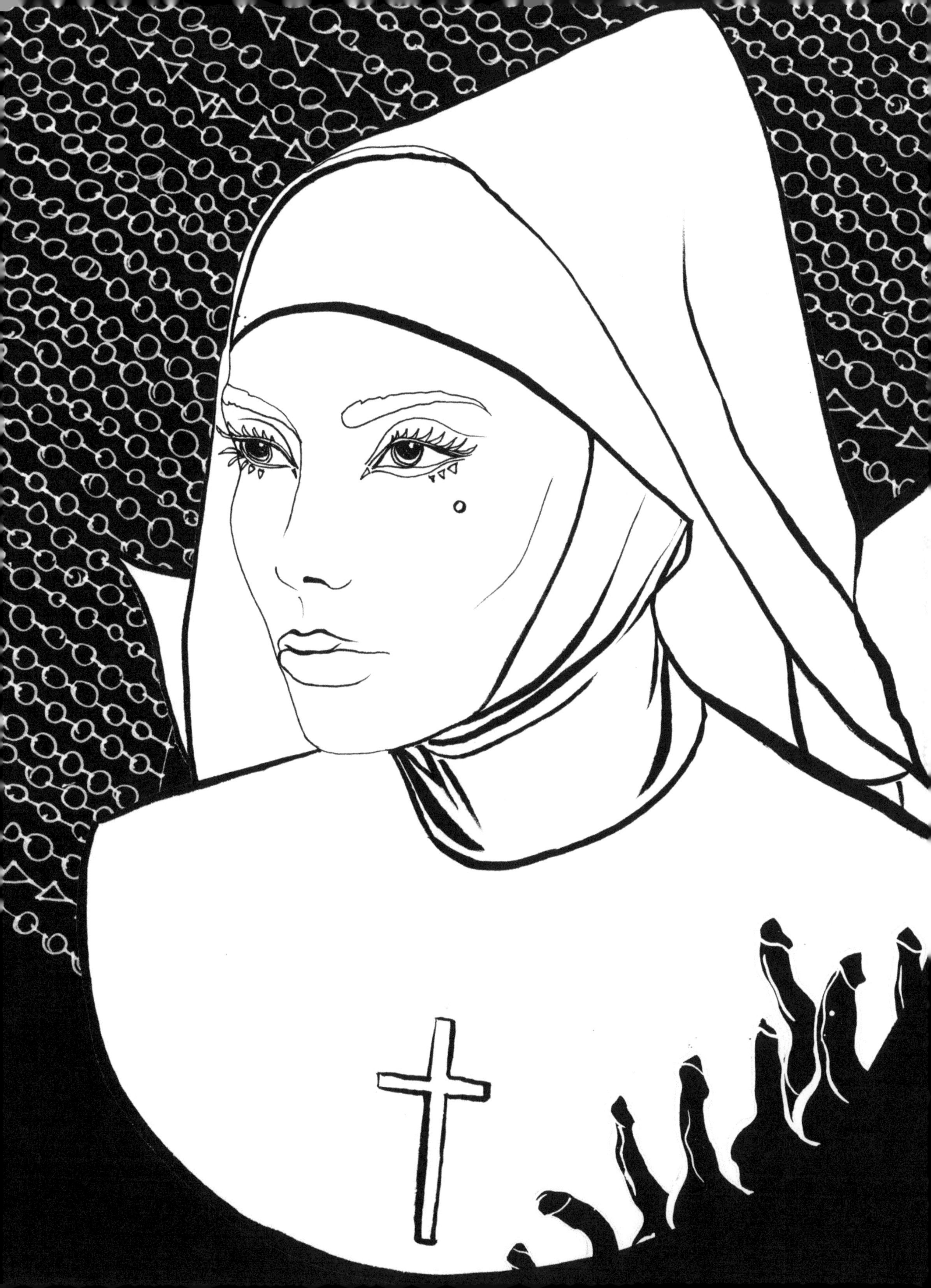

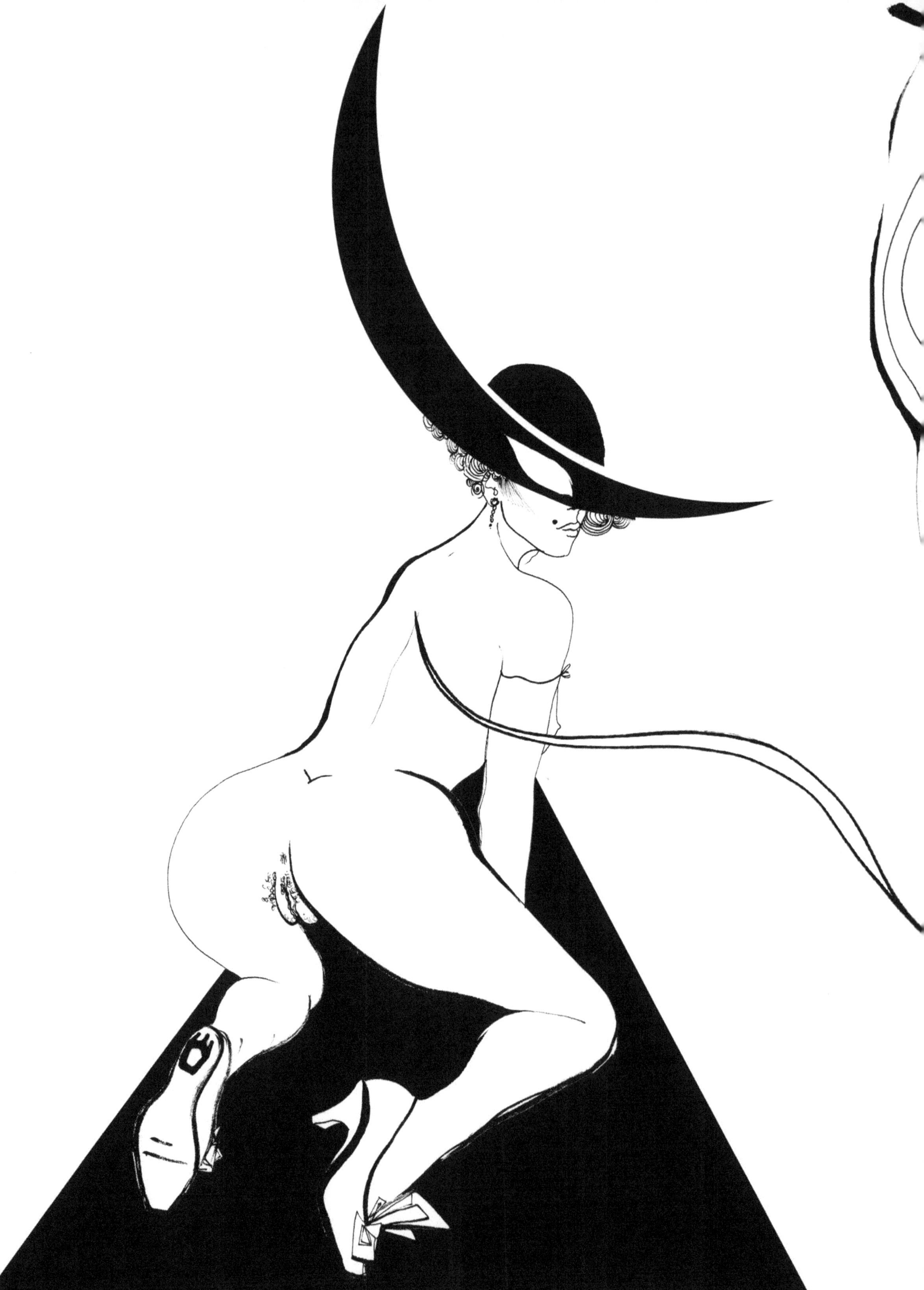

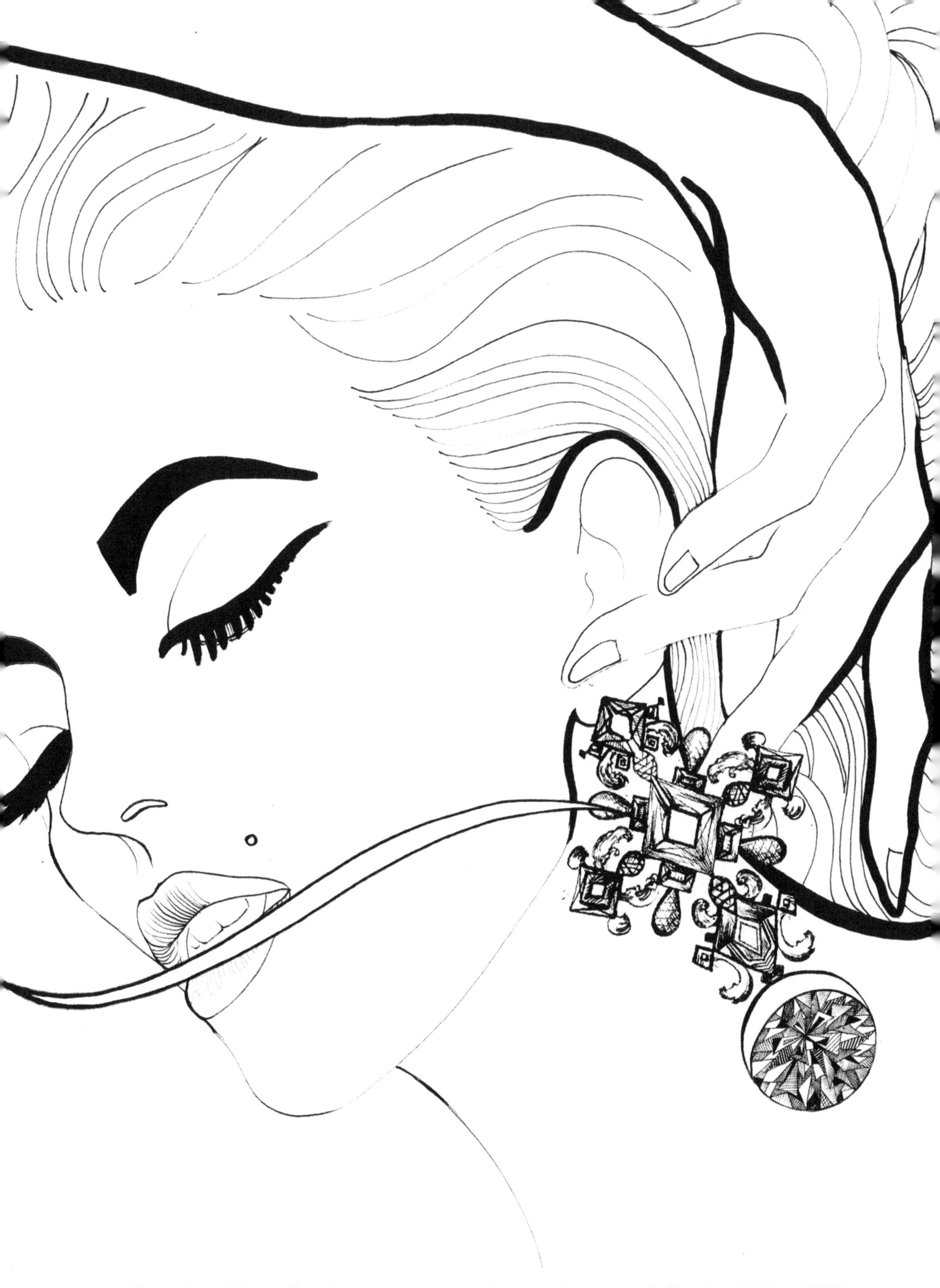

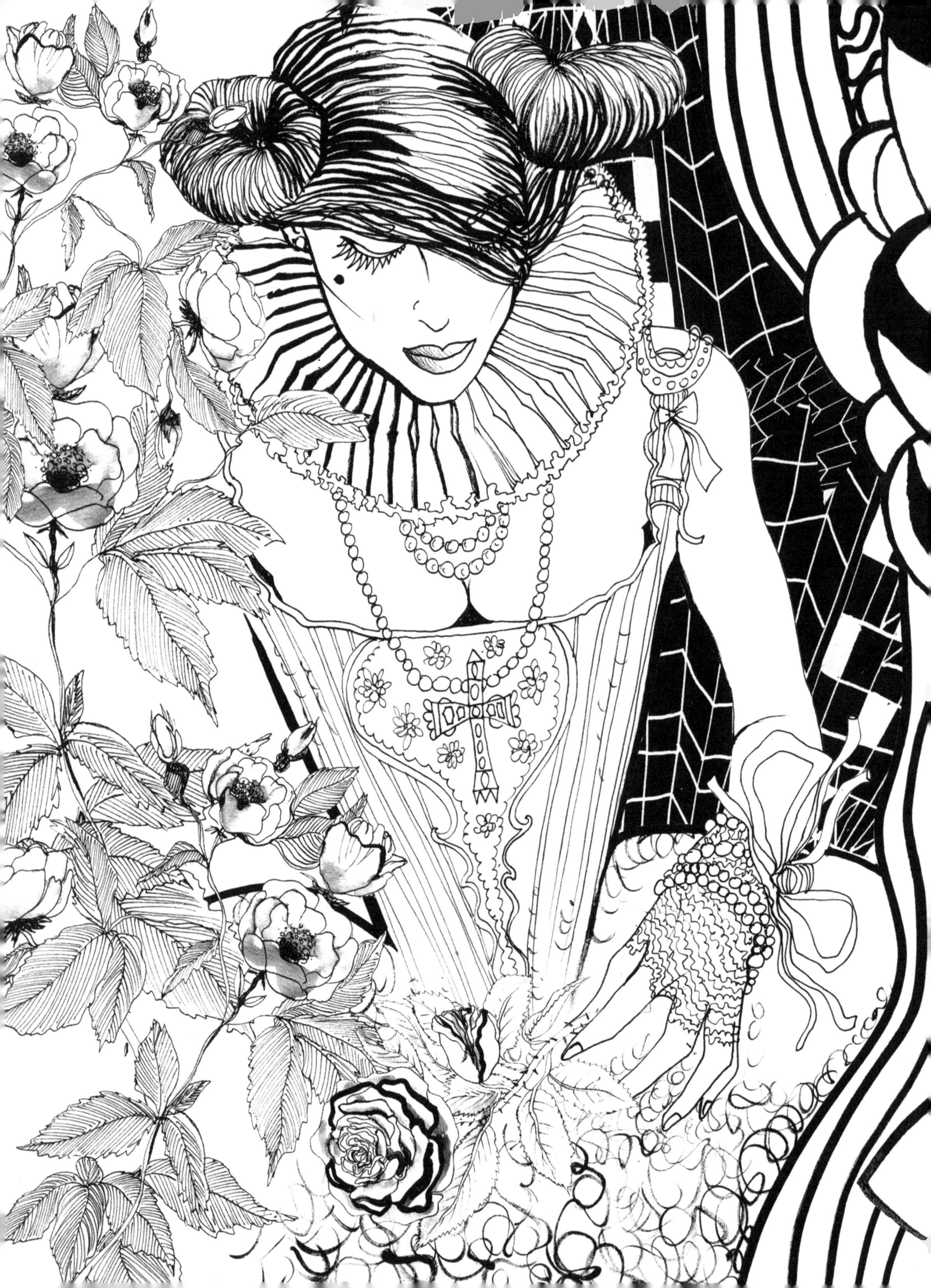

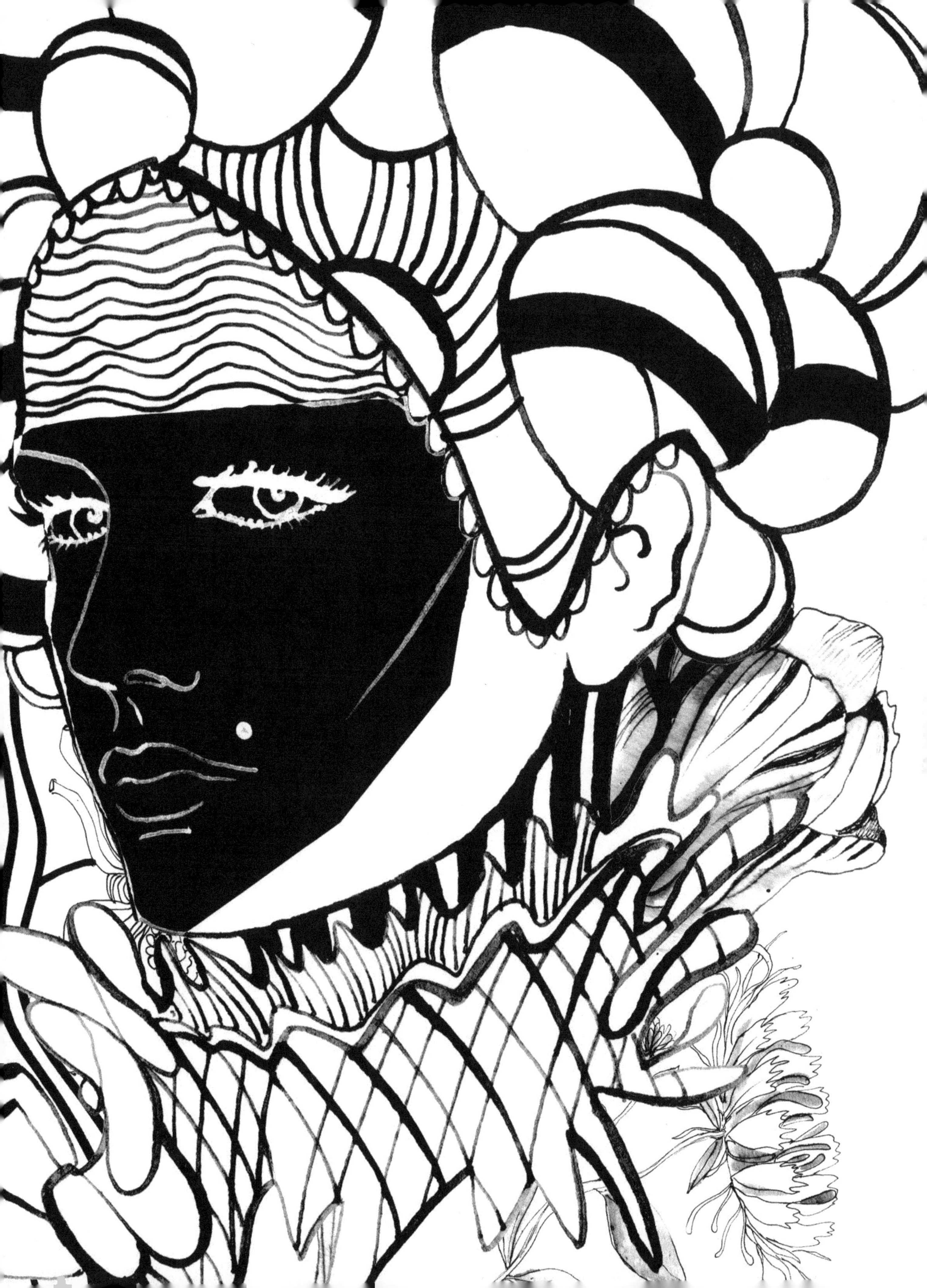

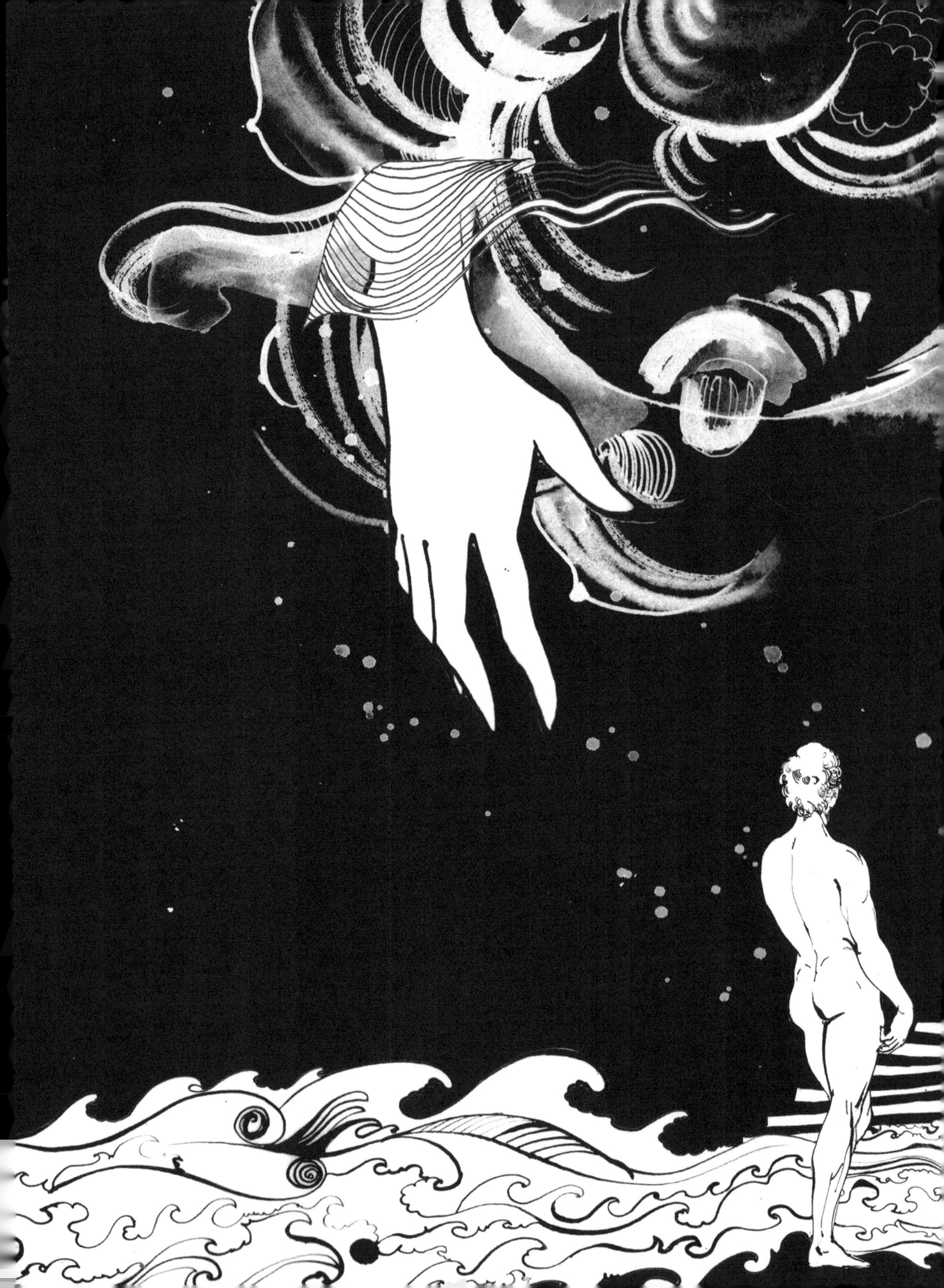

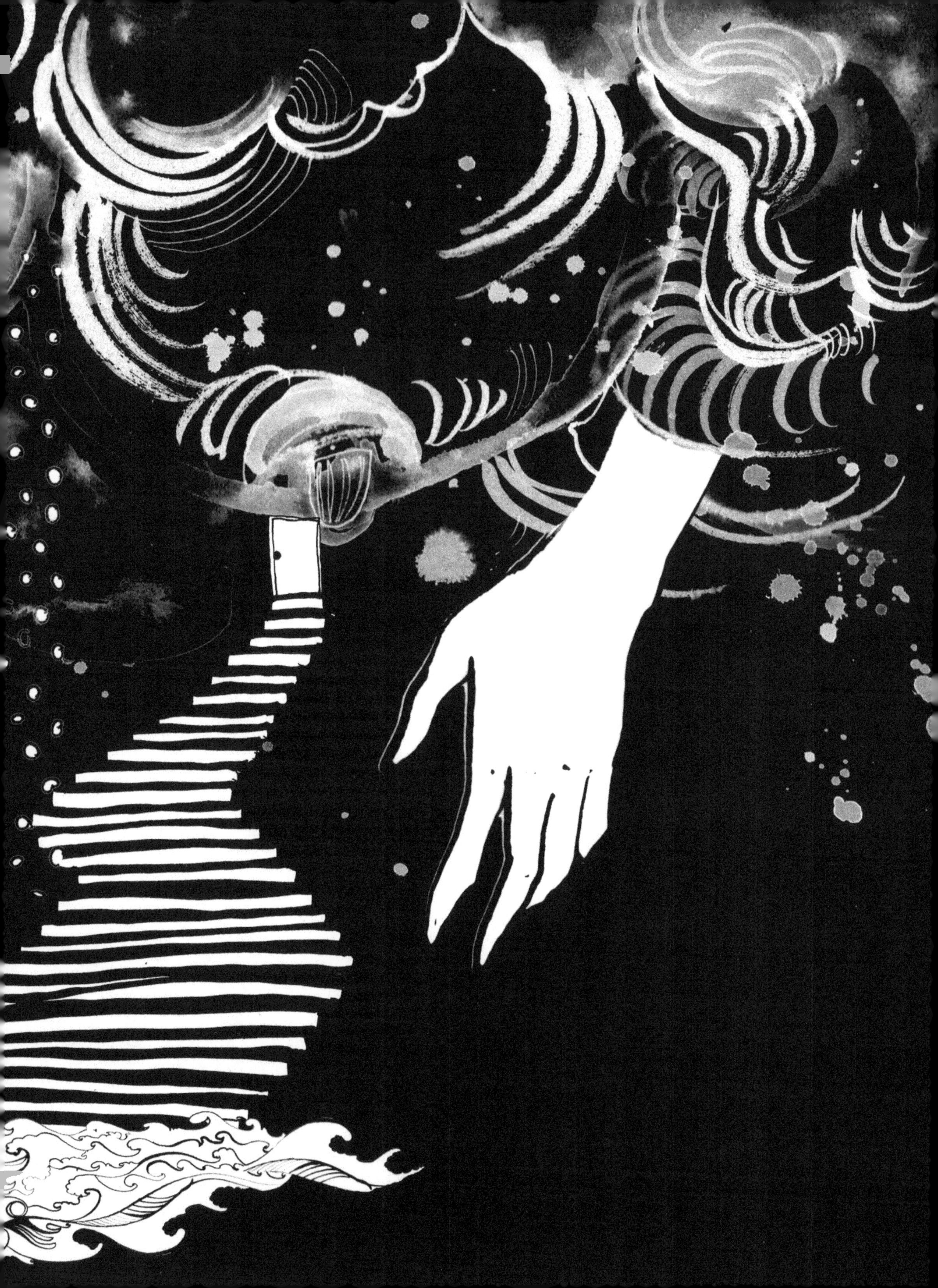

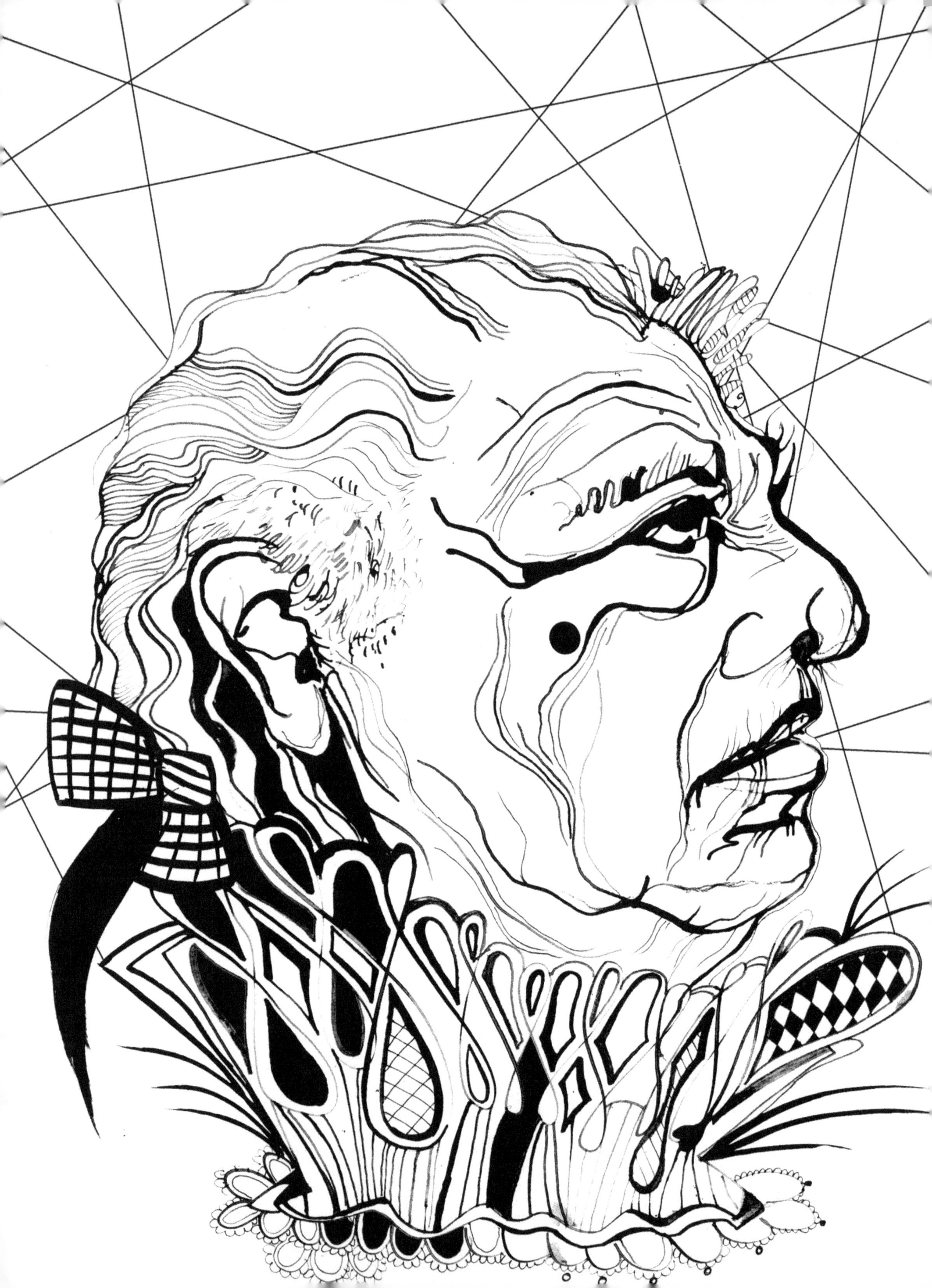

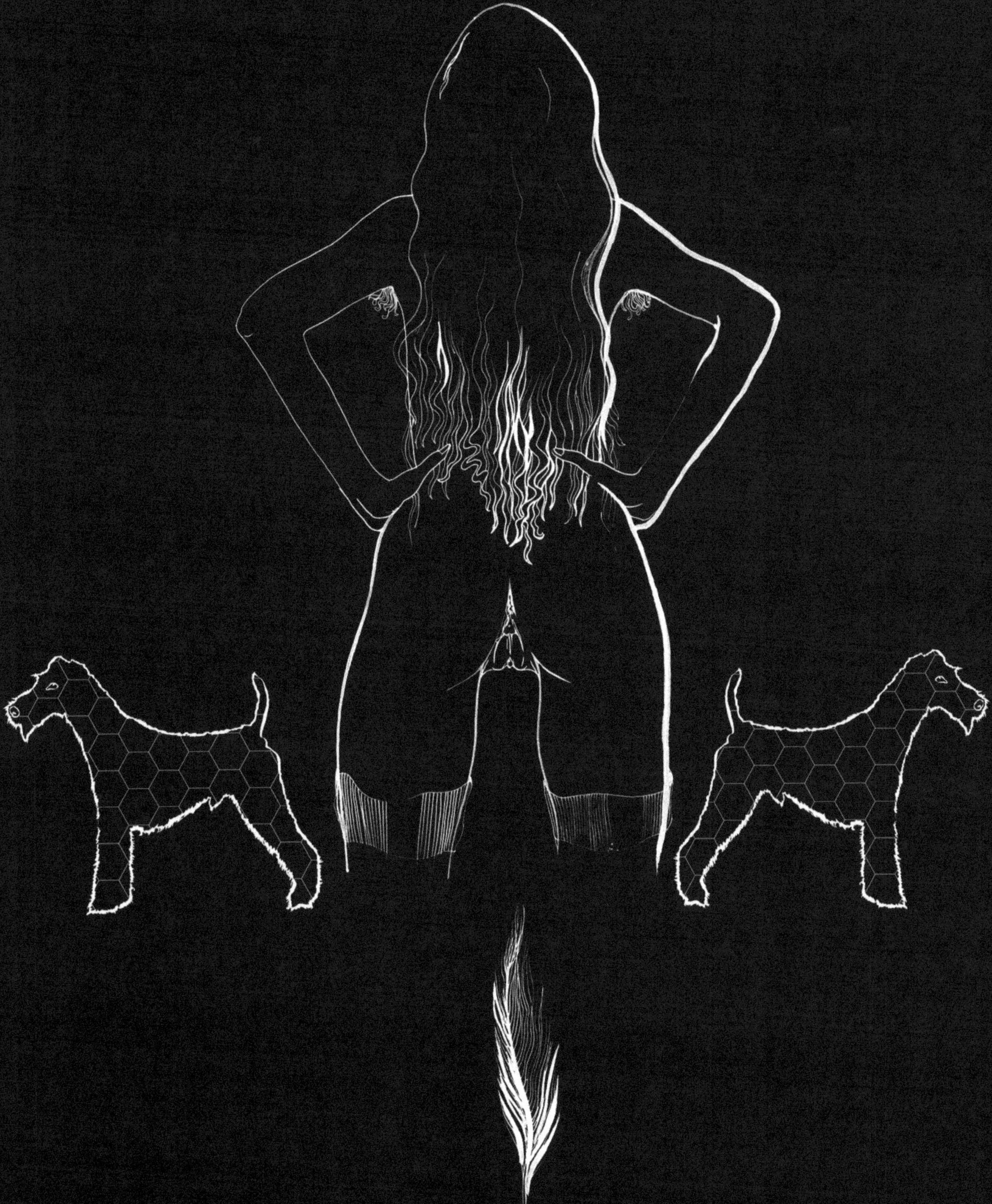

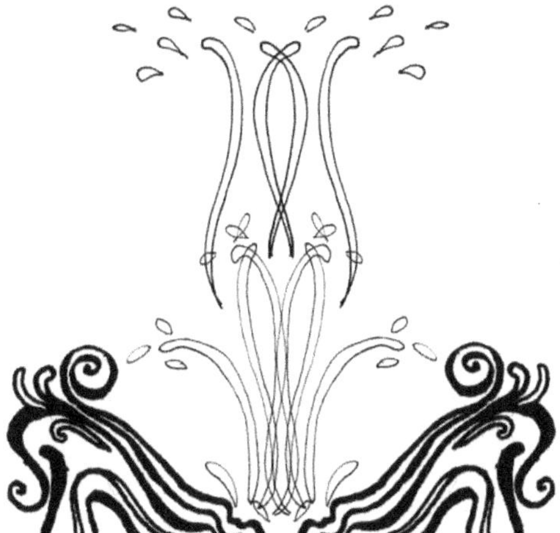

www.ingramcontent.com/pod-product-compliance
Lightning Source LLC
Chambersburg PA
CBHW040547220526
45473CB00017B/3045
* 9 7 8 1 7 3 2 0 0 9 1 8 9 *